How to start a business from home

Emma Jones

HARRIMAN HOUSE LTD
3A Penns Road
Petersfield
Hampshire
GU32 2EW
GREAT BRITAIN
Tel: +44 (0)1730 233870
Fax: +44 (0)1730 233880
Email: enquiries@harriman-house.com
Website: www.harriman-house.com

First published in Great Britain in 2008
Copyright © Harriman House Ltd
The right of Emma Jones to be identified as Author has been
asserted in accordance with the Copyright, Design and Patents Act
1988.
ISBN: 1-905641-68-0
978-1905641-68-0
British Library Cataloguing in Publication Data
A CIP catalogue record for this book can be obtained from the
British Library.

Printed and bound by Cambridge Printing, University Printing
House, Cambridge.
Designed by San Sharma.
Photography by Jill Jennings, taken at Redbrick House with
friends, family and colleagues of Emma Jones.

This book was written in Redbrick House,
my home office in Shropshire.

The pictures were taken in and around the house.
They show me, my family and my homeworking friends.

Contents

Introduction

After five years of working for a multinational corporation, in a job that took me all over the world, I decided to come home.

I was 27. And I wanted, more than anything, to be my own boss, to start my own business and to take control of my lifestyle.

So I cleared out the spare room, invested in a new laptop and started to make some calls. That was the beginning of 'Techlocate', an inward investment consultancy that grew to employing 5 people in home offices in London and Manchester. Two years after start-up, I successfully sold the business to the sort of corporation I'd left behind.

Then I launched a website to help people do what I did – to start and grow a business from home. It's become the largest site of its kind in the UK and has spawned a home business video show too. I manage the site, run the business and record the show from Redbrick House, my homely head office in Shropshire.

"Along the way, I've learned some valuable lessons and made some incredible friends. And I'd like to share with you some of my experiences."

Along the way, I've learned some valuable lessons and made some incredible friends. And I'd like to share with you some of my experiences.

So, as you embark on your own journey, to start a home business and lead a balanced life, I hope you'll find this a useful guide.

Happy homeworking!
Emma Jones

Why start a home business?

If you have this book, you're probably thinking about starting a home business. And I say to you, good idea!

There are over 2 million home businesses in the UK and more than 60% of all businesses are started at home. Add to that the 1,400 new home businesses that are started each week and you get the idea:

You are not alone!

Starting a home business means you can save money and time. Why rent an office when your spare room, your kitchen table or even your shed can do the job just as well – actually, even better?

The average commuter will travel two and a half times around the world during the course of their working life. So, if yours is a 60 second commute to the home office desk, imagine the savings you can make in time and money. Probably enough for a round-the-world trip!

But the first journey you'll take is with me. Over the following pages, you'll meet my friends and family and get a good look inside my working home! With this book, you'll be up and running in no time. And once you are, you can start to enjoy the benefits of working from home.

Benefits such as being able to spend more time and energy doing the things you enjoy, whilst earning an income, and without being stuck in traffic or in an office block somewhere.

Every journey begins with a small step. Buying this book was your first.

Are you ready for the next step?

" The average commuter will travel two and a half times around the world during the course of their working life. "

Business

1. Finding the right idea

It all begins with an idea. Or so said Archimedes, Newton, and Edison. But in this chapter I'm going to show you that you don't need to slip in the bath or be hit on the head by an apple (or anything, for that matter). Sometimes you already have the idea. You just need to coax it out.

5 tips for 'coaxing out' an idea

1. Hobby horse riding.
Think of the things you like to do best and that make full use of your skills and talent. It could be a hobby or a favourite pastime. In any case, pick from the list the thing you think you can sustain most interest in, because, if you're going to build a home business around it, it needs to be able to hold your interest.

2. Mind the gap!
It's not just good advice when boarding the Tube, it's also a great way to spot a business opportunity. Think of a time when you've wanted to buy or use something but you just can't find it in the shops or in the Yellow Pages. Can you fill this gap in the market with your business idea?

3. Anything you can do I can do better.
If you've been disappointed by a product or service, why not try to channel your frustrations into your own solution?

That's what Julie Bishop did, and she's now running 'Living Clean' as a successful home business.

"The idea came about when I was looking for home cleaning products that didn't contain any harsh chemicals," Julie says. "When I couldn't find any, I realised that there must be a gap in the market in creating an alternative way to clean peoples homes. I started to work for a couple of agencies, but it wasn't long before I realised I could do it better myself! That was six months ago and the phone hasn't stopped ringing since!"

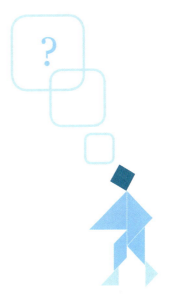

Elod Beregszaszi

Elod Beregszaszi, Popupology

"My business came about almost by accident! When I was made redundant from a part-time job in a bookshop, I chanced upon turning a lifelong passion for origami, and all things paper, into a way of making a living.

"Popupology is the name I chose for my home business, and I suppose I would describe myself as a paper-engineer and designer, creating pop-up templates for paper sculptures, cards, window displays and a lot else besides."

Elod's business involved market testing and getting to know suppliers for a year before starting out as a sole trader at the end of 2006. His first step was to launch a small range of origami architecture cards, working from home as a "kitchen table publisher" folding and gluing the designs by hand.

"I've been fortunate in that I get more and more work through referrals, one commission leading to another, but I've also embarked on a hectic social life, meeting as many people as I can, which actually turned out to be the best thing about self-employment. It's a lot of fun and work at the same time. Joining business networks has proved fruitful and I would recommend it to anyone starting out."

The response to Elod's work has been encouraging and he relishes the satisfaction of making creative projects happen: "All things experimental are leaps into the unknown and the bigger the learning curve the greater the sense of achievement. I have also had to accept that making 'mistakes' is part of the process. That has been the most valuable lesson so far and has turned me into an eternal optimist."

4. It's good to talk.

Talk to family and friends and ask them where they think your talents lie. They might just help you discover your business idea in an area you hadn't thought of.

5. All out of ideas?

If you're all out of ideas but desperate to turn that spare room into a home office, why not start with a franchise? There's a good number of quality companies offering this kind of opportunity. Companies like Debutots, My Secret Kitchen, Music Bugs, Virgin Vie and Travel Counsellors, to name a few.

Starting out this way will give you an idea of what it's like to be your own boss, with an already established business idea, plus the support of other franchisees.

- Debutots
  www.debutots.co.uk
- My Secret Kitchen
  www.mysecretkitchen.co.uk
- Music Bugs
  www.musicbugs.co.uk
- Virgin Vie
  www.virginvieathome.com
- Travel Counsellors
  www.travelcounsellors.co.uk

TIP

The Name Game
This may just be your toughest job when starting out: Coming up with a name! Settle down for a night in, collect a pen and paper and start writing.

Try to choose something that's:
- *Simple*
- *Memorable*
- *Not being used by anyone else/is too similar to anyone else's (see 'Name Check' p35)*
- *Has an available domain name, i.e. website address (see 'Choosing a domain' p159)*

The name doesn't have to spell out what you do but if it does it should help your website appear nearer the top of online search results.

Plus, people will instantly understand what you do/offer/sell, which could be useful when first starting out.

Doing your research

Once you've come up with your idea, you'll need to do some research to make sure it makes good business sense. For as rewarding and enjoyable as running a home business is, it also needs to pay the bills!

When researching the viability of your home business idea, ask yourself these questions:

How big is the market?

Many home business owners have found their fortunes with ideas that appeal to niche communities. Those ideas are much easier to market as you're likely to know more about your customers.

I once interviewed a home business owner who sells worms and other supplies to keen gardeners. It may sound like a crazy idea, but Heather Gorringe now turns over £2.5 million from a cow shed on her farm in rural Herefordshire. Heather's home business, Wiggly Wigglers, supplies everything from larvae and worms to straw, compost and seeds.

Her website features an online shop and also acts as a meeting place for this niche community, with gardening guides and a popular podcast, recorded from Heather's "wiggly sofa", that attracts over 30,000 listeners!

The 'niche' community Heather discovered was in pockets everywhere. By joining them together she's built a successful home business – and now takes orders from all over the world!

10 business ideas that you can do at home

1. Journalism
2. Design
3. Arts & crafts
4. Hairdressing
5. eBay seller
6. Accounting
7. Law
8. Pet grooming
9. Tuition
10. Catering

5 business ideas that you can't do at home

1. Race car driving
2. Space exploration
3. Deep sea drilling
4. Industrial manufacture
5. Whaling

Gina Krupski, Pink Camellia

Having spent 8 years in Warsaw on account of her husband's job, Gina Krupski returned to the UK in late 2004 and decided she'd get back into her profession as an accountant. But it wasn't to be. She was over 50 and hadn't worked for ten years. After writing many letters Gina realised she was no longer the desirable commodity she'd been in her earlier days and was going to have to find some other form of employment.

"The stark truth was that the only person who would employ me was me and I was forced to start thinking of what I could possibly do for myself.

"I was trying to replace a dressing gown and started to search but couldn't find anything in a high quality fabric or stylish design. I decided to do some research and find out if there was a gap in this market. There was!"

It didn't take Gina long to settle on the brands she wanted to stock. She found silks from Italy, unusual kimono robes from Paris, gorgeous mules and lots of high quality classic nightwear.

She decided to call the business Pink Camellia, in honour of her mother and the beautiful plants she'd inherited from her garden.

"I did many courses at the local college which were extremely useful. There were so many subjects on which I was almost completely ignorant and there was a course on almost all of them; there was even one about how to start up an ecommerce business ... perfect for me."

It took Gina nine months to go from her original idea to launching the Pink Camellia website. Orders started coming in immediately.

"At the age of 51, I'm modelling collections at Charity fashion shows, appearing in the press and exhibiting at large consumer fairs. I'm also feeling the sheer fun of being part of the working population again. It has been a wonderful experience which has certainly given me the opportunity to try something that I have always wanted to do – be my own boss!"

> "The stark truth was that the only person who would employ me was me... I was forced to think of what I could do for myself."

What will you charge?

How much do you think customers or clients would pay for your product or service? Take a look at how similar offerings are priced and talk to people about how much they'd be willing to pay.

Then talk to suppliers to check you can source materials and deliver at a price that covers your costs. Once you've found your price point, make sure you're happy you can reach it and still make a profit.

Remember, since starting a home business will save you lots of money, you can pass some of these savings onto your customers. It will give you an edge over other businesses. But don't undercharge for the expertise and knowledge you offer.

Also consider charging less for work that will reflect well on your home business and boost your reputation, perhaps in the newspaper or with a credible customer.

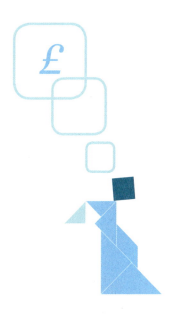

What are others doing?

Take a look at other businesses that have similar ideas. See what they offer and what sort of response they get from their customers. You can do most of this on the Internet. Visit competitor websites and, better still, Internet forums where you think your potential customers might post comments (good and bad) about the competition. It's also worth buying from your competitors, or using their service, so you can get an idea of their strong points – and maybe their weaknesses too.

Once you've answered these questions, it's helpful to do what's called a SWOT analysis.

It stands for Strengths, Weaknesses, Opportunities and Threats. Analysing these things really makes you think about your idea and gives you the confidence to head in the right direction.

SWOT Analysis

These are the questions that I ask myself in my own personal SWOT Analysis.

Strengths
What are my strengths?
- What can I do better than anyone else?
- What resources do I have?
- What's my unique selling point (USP)?

Weaknesses
What are my weaknesses?
- What should I avoid?
- Where do I lack skills?
- What might hinder my success?

Opportunities
What opportunities do I see?
- Does my idea tap into any trends?
- Are there any emerging technologies that could help my idea?
- Has there been anything in the news related to my idea?

Threats
What are the threats?
- What's my competition?
- Does changing technology affect my idea?

SWAP Analysis

Once you've done that you can do what I call a SWAP analysis. Swap your idea for a few minutes of your family and friends' time. Ask plenty of questions and listen to their feedback.

You can do all of this without quitting your day job. That'll take away some of the risk of starting a home business and means you can continue to keep putting money aside until you're ready.

That's what I did and many of the home business owners I know did the same. I gave up my day job only when I was ready to make the move. This contributes to what's being called the "5pm 'til 9am" economy...with lots of people building up their business in their spare time during evenings and at weekends!

Andrew Innes, PortrayIt

Andrew runs a canvas printing company called PortrayIt. While the business was still growing, Andrew continued to study at university, moving his home office between his dorm room and his parents' house. He still hasn't quit his day job – of being a student! – but is supplementing his student loan with the earnings from his online shop and newly opened retail unit.

Andrew started painting pop art on canvas as a hobby. This caught the attention of his friends and family and then a wider audience, but making a profit was difficult, even though Andrew could see a promising business opportunity.

"So I decided to turn my hobby into a business. With my own money and some help from my family I invested in a large format canvas printer to reproduce artwork more quickly. This allowed me to make canvases of the customers' own photographs and became lucrative very quickly.

"When I started my business, working from home was the only real option. The initial costs for equipment and materials were high enough without having to worry about renting premises. I converted the garage into a home office, which left me enough room for all my equipment."

Andrew now has a retail unit too, but all of his online orders and admin work is done from the home office. He says that working from home has allowed him a flexible lifestyle, which means he can run the business whilst doing a degree course.

"When I'm at uni, I basically have to take the office with me, including all my equipment and enough materials to last through term. At first, it posed a bit of an unwelcome challenge, but I soon got used to it. At the moment, I'm training someone to run the retail unit whilst I'm away. That means I can concentrate on my online orders (and my university degree, of course!). If I wasn't running a business, I'd probably be doing my degree, whilst surviving on my student loan and a part-time job!"

2. Making a plan

Home business owners rarely leap for joy at the prospect of writing – or even reviewing – their business plan.

That's because the idea of doing it is a lot worse than actually doing it. Once you get beyond the mindset that writing a business plan is a monumental task, you'll find that it's a lot easier than you thought – and you'll feel so good once it's done!

Getting started

Think about planning your business like you would plan a holiday. You might think the two are incompatible! But they needn't be...

Let's say you're planning to go on a roadtrip. You'll need a starting point and an end point, a map, and a list of things to see and do on the way. And, of course, you'll need resources – fuel for the car, snacks for the journey, etc.

Making a plan for your business is not that different. It'll act as a map, to guide your business from start to growth and you can set milestones for the things you want to achieve. For example, you might want to launch a website or reach a certain number of customers.

It'll also include information about how you intend to get started and what your objectives are. You might want to start a business to sell it in a few years time. Or grow to a point where you wouldn't want to grow anymore.

And, of course, you'll need to refer to resources: what you have already, what you'll need and how you'll pay for it.

But there's one big difference between planning a holiday and planning a business. There's a cost involved with each, certainly. But on holiday you can only spend money, whereas in business you can make a whole lot of it!

TIP

Phone a friend
Could one of your friends be your business partner? Think carefully about whether you want to start and grow the business on your own (and have full control), or with someone else?

If you decide to start a partnership with a friend, look for someone with different but complementary skills and a shared vision.

Business plan

After coming up with an idea, writing your business plan is your first practical step to starting your home business. With it under your belt you can say, "I'm off!"

Or IMOFF.

It's an easy way to remember the headings to include in your business plan: Idea, Market, Operations, Financials and Friends.

Idea
What's your idea?

Market
Who will be your customers or clients? And what is your competition in the same area?

Operations
How will you develop your idea, promote it and take care of existing clients or customers?

Financials
Does it all add up? How will you keep from spending more than you earn? Can you earn enough to live on, and support any dependents?

Friends
Who can you turn to for regular business advice? Are there other home businesses that are complementary to yours? Can you share marketing opportunities? Contacts and experience?

> **TIP**
>
> **IMOFF**
> - Idea
> - Market
> - Operations
> - Financials
> - Friends

The 'F' word

Another 'F' word really worth remembering is funding. Where will the money that you need to start up come from?

Don't worry! It may cost a lot less than you think. You probably already have a computer and a mobile phone, so you might not need to buy much more equipment (depending on your business). And think of the money you'll save being based at home: No premises, no commute, no overpriced sandwiches at lunchtime...!

Check out my home office shopping list to see how you can be up and running for under £500. The only thing you'll need to add in is the cost of any start-up stock.

TIP

__Home office shopping list__
Starting out for under £500.

It's cheaper than buying two first class rail tickets from Manchester to London!

1 x desk

1 x chair

1 x laptop

1 x broadband package

1 x domain name

1 x 500 business cards

1x bottle of bubbly to celebrate!

1 x job satisfaction

£36

£13.99

£335.99

£14.99

£8.75

£49

£19.99

Priceless!

Total

£478.71

Places to look for funding

If you think you'll need funding all the same, here are a few places to look.

Friends and family

Friends and family are people you can trust – and asking them for money hopefully won't come with strings attached! Do consider though having a written agreement that covers the amount borrowed and a payback schedule.

The bank

High street banks are falling over themselves to appear the most friendly to small business owners. Make the most of their enthusiasm and ask to speak to a small business advisor at your local branch. Take a copy of your business plan with you and be prepared to talk through it.

Credit cards

Many a home business has been started with help from a flexible friend! Again, shop for the best rates. It's a competitive market and the credit card companies are keen for your business. Be on time with repayments (to avoid penalty interest charges) and aim to pay back the credit as soon as you can and as sales start coming in.

TIP

Opening a bank account

Shop around for the best rates and deals (you can do this online through comparison sites) and open an account early on so you don't mix up your business and personal finances, which may complicate record keeping.

Grants

There are grants available from a number of sources, including the government, European Union, Regional Development Agencies, Business Link, local authorities and some charitable organisations, such as The Prince's Trust.

Find out more about grants and other help that may be available to you at:

- Business Link
  www.businesslink.gov.uk
- J4b Grants
  www.j4bgrants.co.uk

Investors

Angel investors and venture capitalists can help raise large amounts of start-up funding or development capital for businesses looking to grow. It might be an idea to consider this route further down the line. It doesn't have to be a gruesome experience though (think of TV show *Dragons' Den*) as there are plenty of funds and investors out there, eager to part with their money and back good ideas.

- Angels Den
  www.angelsden.co.uk

TIP

Places to look for funding
Down the side of the sofa?
Well, you never know what you'll find!

(This business plan is for a 2 year cycle. You may choose to do a 12 month plan, or up to 5 years!)

Contents
Executive Summary •
The Idea •
The Market •
Operations •
Friends & Family •
Financials •

Executive Summary

Summarise what's in the rest of the plan. Something like this:

The vision for ABC is to become the leading company for selling xxx to xxx. This plan sets out how the vision will be achieved in the period from 2008-2010. It outlines the product on offer, provides data on the customer market and shows how an experienced founder will have the company operating profitably within the first 3 months.

Having identified a clear gap in the market, I'm excited about the opportunity to start and build a successful business that will offer a quality product and service to a well defined market.

A. Smith
Founder, Company ABC

The Idea

Include here your 'elevator pitch'; what is your product and how will it benefit the customer.

The Market

Customers
Who will be your customers; include the number of them, their demographic profile, geographic location, social and education background; essentially any strong data that shows you know your audience.

Competition
Who is selling a similar product/service. How do you differ from them and what is your unique selling point.

You can do this by producing a table that lists the competition and you. Outline what makes you stand out in the market; is it that your service will be online, that you'll charge a different price, have an innovative marketing approach or offer the service with a special extra twist?

Operations

The CEO
You have come up with the idea for the business and you've done your research on the market. Now it's time for the reader to know a bit about you! Note your background, skills, experience and any credentials for running this business.

Sourcing
If this applies to your business, refer to how you'll source your product/service. You may be making it yourself!

Business plan example

Use this template to write your own business plan.

Sales & Marketing

How will you promote what you offer to your customers. Include a brief sales and marketing plan with headings like this:

- Press — how many press releases do you plan to distribute each year and to which press channels; newspapers, magazines, radio, etc.
- Online — will you have your own blog/website? Mention other sites that you'll approach for reciprocal links
- Partners — what about marketing tie-ups with other companies selling to the same audience

You know where your customers are so let your marketing plan show that you'll reach them in print, online and even in the streets!

Most home business owners I know have started the business with their own money and written business plans for their own ends. Preparing a plan helps you see the business clearly and chart your course with confidence.

Systems

You've sourced the service/product and told customers about it. Refer here to the process customers will go through to buy from you and the systems you'll have in place to deliver in time and on budget. Systems that may include online ordering & payment, a professional call handling service to take orders or maybe some specific software.

Friends & Family

In starting and growing your home based business, will you call on friends & family for advice? If so, refer to this here; mention your board of advisors, your experts-on-call, your support network!

Financials

Last but not least come the figures. Make this as basic as possible and it's probably best to do it in table form:

	Year 1	Year 2
Revenue	xxxx	xxxx
Overheads		
• Office rent	0	0
• Salary	(xx)	(xx)
• Stock	(xx)	(xx)
• Technology	(xx)	(xx)
• Marketing	(xx)	(xx)
• Travel & expenses	(xx)	(xx)
Projected profit	xxxx	xxxx

Drawing up a simple financial forecast will highlight any need to borrow money or look for funding.

Registration Time

Once the planning's done, you'll need to register your new business with a couple of organisations. Just like a newborn baby has a birth certificate to recognise date of birth and parentage, your new company needs certifying too!

The first registration is with Companies House, but before getting in touch, have a think about the company status that suits you best.

- Companies House
  www.companieshouse.gov.uk

Sole trader
Being a sole trader is the simplest way to start and run a home business. You keep records and accounts of your own activity and, in acting alone, get to keep all the profits!

Partnership
If you'd like to be self-employed but want to work with a friend or colleague, consider a partnership. It means that two or more people share the risks, costs, and workload!

Limited company

Limited companies exist in their own right, with the company's finances kept separate from the personal finances of its owners.

The status of your company will affect how much admin you have to do and the kind of financial records to keep and file. Take advice from your accountant or local tax office on which one to choose.

When registering, there are two options. You can buy a 'ready-made' company from a company formation agent, or you can 'incorporate' a company yourself by sending documents and a registration fee to Companies House.

Brand protection

There's also a matter of 'intellectual property'. This may involve registering a trademark or, if you've come up with a unique invention a patent. Registering either means companies can't come along and use your name or invention, without your permission.

- UK Intellectual Property Office
  www.ipo.gov.uk

TIP

Name check
When coming up with a name for your company, visit the Companies House website to check you're not registering the same name as another company or using words you shouldn't be using!

Value Added Tax (VAT)

TIP

Get help
Unless you're a bit
of a whiz when it
comes to company
set-up and accounts,
consider hiring a local
accountant at this
point.

Make sure they're
registered with the
Institute of Chartered
Accountants in
England & Wales
and ask friends
and local business
owners for their
recommendations. If
you think you can't
afford this service, tot
up how much time it
would take you to do
this work and how
much you could earn in
that time.

If that's more than
what the accountant
quotes, hire them and
take it off your to do
list!

Will you be registering for VAT with HM Revenue & Customs? It's worth bearing in mind the pros and cons.

Being VAT registered can give your home business credibility with certain customers and when you charge VAT, you can claim back the VAT you've already paid, which can result in a credit.

On the other hand, if you include VAT in your pricing it may make you more expensive than your competitors and you'll have to submit a VAT return four times a year, which adds to your admin 'to do' list.

In any case, if your home business turns over a certain amount of money you'll have to register for VAT. You can find out more on the Business Link website and register for VAT online with HM Revenue & Customs.

- Business Link
  www.businesslink.gov.uk/taxes
- HM Revenue & Customs
  www.hmrc.gov.uk

Your tax position

Your tax position will change when you become self-employed and there's benefit in being a home-based business.

Personal tax

The amount of personal tax you pay will depend on how much you choose to pay yourself and on your company status. You can claim work-related travel as an expense, which reduces your tax bill and is something regular commuters can't claim.

Corporate tax

The amount of corporate tax you pay depends on how much your home business turns over. You can also claim home office-related expenses, such as furnishings and a portion of your heating, lighting and electricity bill. These will reduce your tax bill.

Speak to your local tax office or accountant about the positive tax impact.

* HM Revenue & Customs
  www.hmrc.gov.uk

3. Sales and marketing

There comes a point in every home business owners' career when thinking must turn into doing.

Once you've thought of an idea and written your business plan, focus your energy on reaching out to your first customer or client.

Think of it as one small step for you, one giant leap for your home business. You'll be over the moon when you make your first sale!

Here's how to do it.

Making your first sale

1. Make a list (check it twice)

Draw on your existing resources, grab your address book and circle the friends, family, colleagues and acquaintances you think might be interested in your product or service. Add to the list with details of local people and businesses too.

2. Pitch up

Write to the people on your list and announce your new business venture. Consider this an opportunity to make your pitch, but don't be too pushy. And remember to address each recipient personally. No one likes a group e-mail!

3. Follow up

Follow up in a few days time, either with another e-mail or, better still, a phone call. Take some soundings as to the success of your pitch and react accordingly. If the potential customer or client sounds keen, go for it! Arrange to meet him or her to show your product or explain more about your service.

4. Meet up

Arrange a time and place to meet that's convenient for your potential customer or client. Be professional, but also likeable. They're equally important characteristics when making a sale.

If the customer agrees the deal, bring the meeting to a fairly speedy end. Your job is done – for now. It's time to head home and deliver on the promise you made with your first customer.

5. Make some noise

Once you've made your first sale – shout about it! If your new customer or client agrees, include them in a press release or write about them on your website or blog, so other potential customers or clients can see that you're well and truly in business!

TIP

Hello!
When you make a sales call, stand up and smile. It will make you sound confident and positive.

Marketing your home business

Don't stop at one sale! You need to keep up the momentum, keep selling and keep growing that list of potential customers. Follow these steps to market your home business and increase sales.

Write the script
Imagine yourself as the star of your own Hollywood movie. Are you an action hero, battling against the odds (think James Dyson) or a brand leading lady (think Nigella Lawson)? Plot the action and write the script. It will help you define your message to the media.

Friend of a friend
Research the journalists you think are interested in your field. Note their email addresses from the bottom of their articles, get to know them and send them exclusive stories about you and your home business.

Become an expert
Set yourself up as an expert in your field and the media will come to you. Do this by sharing your knowledge via a blog, write a report, make predictions or write a book.

This is what Stuart Payne did. He became an international expert on tea and biscuits, when publishers noticed the attention his blog, www.nicecupofteaandasitdown.com, was getting and offered him a book deal. He now makes regular appearances on television and radio, in between tasting tea and biscuits, from his home office in Cambridge.

TIP

The art of networking

A great way to market yourself and your business is to step out of the home office and attend events. But go in prepared. There is an art to networking.

- *Wear your name tag (if you have one) on your right side. It's easy to catch sight of when you are shaking hands*
- *Deliver a nice firm handshake and make eye contact*
- *Say your name clearly and, in under 10 seconds, tell the other person who you are and what you do*
- *Listen carefully. Ask the other person plenty of questions about their line of business, their family, their hobbies*
- *Be positive and energetic*
- *Swap business cards*
- *Send a "thank you" email after the event, confirming any actions you and they have promised*
- *Keep in regular, and meaningful, contact*

Be everywhere

Keep in touch with existing customers via a newsletter and reach out to the new by making regular appearances at events, on other people's websites and blogs, in newspapers and magazines, and on radio and TV.

Write to the magazines and radio stations that ask people to send in their story. It's a free way to get coverage. The more you're covered, the more you'll be invited to speak and comment, and before you know it, you'll be everywhere!

Nula Shearing, Noolibird
Nula Shearing's story is of family fortunes. Her business, Noolibird, was started with help from her mum and dad, husband and auntie, all of whom appear in press releases and promotional photographs!

The story of the family that's working together to grow a home business and support the local economy is great. It's intrinsic to Nula's business, helps customers relate and – importantly – the press take notice.

The Noolibird office and warehouse are nestled under the South Downs in the village of Firle, where Nula spent her childhood, and also where much of the inspiration for Noolibird came from. Animals, nature and fairy stories were big influences in Nula's childhood and were the inspiration for her four collections of designs for children's rooms.

Nula studied textile design at Winchester School of Art, worked as an in-house designer for Jane Churchill for three years and then continued to work as a freelance designer after having her two sons. But when her younger son started nursery school, Nula was ready for a new challenge.

Her Mum was enthusiastic to help in getting her started and as Nula designed the collection, her Mum worked on costings and researching suppliers, using the experience she'd gathered from running her own business.

"I had found it difficult to find imaginative designs for my own children's rooms and had noticed how the market seemed to be flooded with TV character themed bedding; I had a feeling that there may be a gap in the market for a more imaginative and creative approach. I also wanted to be self-employed so that I could  *fit my working hours around being a mum. With the help of a panel of small experts and their parents, I got to work producing designs that would feed young imaginations, in much the same way as a good bedtime story."*

Nula produced a small brochure with the help of her husband, who is a photographer, and a friend's husband designed the first Noolibird website.

"We are driving customers to the website using PR campaigns and encouraging customers to tell their friends. I'm now working on an email campaign to sell new products to existing customers."

The company employs 3 local people; one of whom is Nula's auntie who helps with bookkeeping and another is her cousin, Tom.

"My Mum continues to help me with the day-to-day running and together we pride ourselves on the fast, friendly and family-oriented service that it is possible to offer as a small company."

Press means prizes

Enter awards and competitions and enjoy the press coverage that goes with it. Winning will give you even more press, credibility, oh, and a prize!

Last year, I presented Wendy Shand of Tots to France with a Home Business Award, which Wendy says was good for her confidence and the profile of her business. She was pretty delighted with all the prizes too!

Use a thousand words

When a picture speaks a thousand words you can afford to talk less! Consider hiring a professional photographer to take pictures of you and your work. Maybe you can do this as a barter deal? Or pick up your own digital camera and do it yourself. Use the images on your website and in promotion materials and let your business speak for itself.

TIP

Spoilt for choice
Consider subscribing to an image library. I use istockphoto.com for copyright-free images. It's a pay-as-you-go service with thousands of images and is easy to use.

CASE STUDY

Isobel Davies

Isobel Davies, Izzy Lane
When Isobel Davies started a business from her home, she didn't know that a year later she'd be leading a successful clothing brand and able to say that she's rescued 600 sheep.

Isobel's company, Izzy Lane, is receiving rapturous attention from the media for its line of high quality clothing and its business model of saving sheep that have slight imperfections and would have been sent for slaughter. Not only do these sheep live happily ever after in 'The Sheep Sanctuary', they're also providing work for more than 100 home-based knitters!

"I conceived the idea for Izzy Lane in 2002 and did the bulk of the research back then to understand the processes involved, find manufacturers and processors, designers, etc. I made all the contacts and rescued the first 4 or 5 sheep. A family illness and moving house meant that I wasn't able to return to my vision for Izzy Lane until early 2006."

Isobel has been busy ever since. She works from home in an office that overlooks the garden. She's not the only homeworker in the company as the knitters and designers are all home based too.

"Our products are marketed through PR and some advertising. Izzy Lane has such a rich story that it hasn't been too difficult to find journalists who want to write about it and they find us. That said, it's very early days and we're still finding our way and trying to establish our market."

Isobel knew nothing of the fashion industry before she started but she enjoys the challenge.

"I like to do something new and fresh and that I'm passionate about, something that I feel hasn't been done before. Money isn't the motivating factor though it is the thing that demonstrates you have created a successful business."

Polish your window to the world

A website or blog is your window to the outside world. Make sure it's attractive, useful and up-to-date and you'll have people peering in and spreading the word. (Thousands of them!) Check out chapter 10 for pointers on how to launch and develop your home on the web.

Paint the town

Paint your car with your company name and logo and turn heads as you turn corners. Rennae Matthews of The Soap and Bubble Company has done just that. "The bubble machine is our branded VW beetle," she says. "It helps with brand visibility, as well as being an excellent ice breaker."

Stand out

Before you make contact with the press, and start writing your press releases, think about what makes your home business unique and special. Ask yourself, what's the message you want to convey in your press appearances?

Or, if you really want to stand out, do something extraordinary and get noticed. Sally Walton of Carry-a-Bag took photographs of her bags, had them made into postcards (including full contact details on the back) and then mailed them to the magazines and newspapers on her 'hit list'. *Country Living* featured two of her bags and Sally got immediate orders. Bingo!

Make it easy

Make it easy for journalists to write about you by writing the kind of press release that they dream of. Include an attention-grabbing headline, brief but punchy content, an interesting image, facts and figures, quotes, a celebrity endorsement (if you can), and your contact details so they can get in touch if they need to.

Write to me!

My address is at the back of this book, so write to me with your home business stories. I can feature you on my website and pass your name to journalists who regularly get in touch looking for case studies of successful home businesses.

TIP

PR protocol
Writing a press release costs nothing but your time, yet it can generate thousands of pounds worth of publicity. If you're emailing a press release to journalists, write the text in the body of the email and include it in an attachment too. If you don't get a response, follow up!

Example press release

1. *Attention grabbing headline*

2. *The first line is punchy and explains the what, who, why and where of the headline*

3. *Back up the headline and first sentence with facts and figures*

4. *Include a quote from you*

5. *Can you include a quote from someone else? A happy customer, industry expert, or celebrity?*

6. *End with a call to action. Where can people go to find out more/how to download the report/which site to visit to claim a free gift, etc.*

7. *Include 'Notes to Editors' with brief details on you and your company*

8. *Remember to include contact details – your email address and telephone number*

9. *Attach a relevant and interesting image*

1.

Home office adds £25,000 to property value

2.

Research carried out by home business website, Enterprise Nation [www.enterprisenation.com], reveals that having a home office can add thousands to the value of your home.

A comparison of house prices across the UK has confirmed that it really does pay to work from home with increases in property values ranging from the smallest differential of £2,450, through to a whopping £80,000. This is an £80,000 difference in the amount being offered for

3.

two similar houses located in the same area; one with a home office and the other, woefully, without. The average differential between the properties was £25,000; a significant sum.

4.

Emma Jones, founder and editor of Enterprise Nation, said:

"These results show that not only can you save on costs through working from home, you can also earn a significant sum, just through the rise in property value. If you had not thought about starting your business from home before, then think again!"

And it doesn't seem to matter if your office is in the house, or out. The same value-added applies to having a garden office. Nick Hopewell-

5.

Smith, Chairman of Henley Garden Buildings, confirms that having one of his stylish outdoor offices can add anything from 3-5% to the value of a residential property.

With the evidence clearly pointing to the financial benefits of working

6.

from home, what are you waiting for?!

7.

To view a copy of the research, please visit www.enterprisenation.com

Notes

www.enterprisenation.com is the UK's largest online community of home business owners. Founded by successful entrepreneur Emma Jones, the site is a free resource for people starting and growing a business

8.

from home. The combined turnover of home-based businesses is in excess of £364 billion, with the highest growth coming from mums, young people and the over 50s.

The research was carried out by Enterprise Nation and property search agents, Homefinder UK. It compared residential sales prices in various parts of the UK.

For media enquiries, please contact Emma Jones at emma@enterprisenation.com or call (01234) 567 8910.

9.

Making a good impression

Follow our steps to market your home business and potential customers will come knocking on your home office door. Not literally, of course! But it's good to make sure that when they do call, you're ready to answer with a professional welcome.

Phone

It's cheap and sometimes free to get an 0845 local rate number or an 0870 national rate number for your home business. It will hide where you're based and divert your calls to wherever you specify. But beware: sometimes, having such a number – especially with national rates – might put customers off ringing you.

If you use a landline number it's best to have a separate line for your home and your business. It will stop your business calls from being answered by the kids and also give you a chance to escape work calls when you want to.

And these days, you don't need to invest in an actual second line. I use a VoIP (Voice Over Internet Protocol) phone, which uses my broadband internet connection to make and receive calls. My favourite service is Skype. You can find out more about this on page 142.

- Skype
  www.skype.com

Address

There are a couple of reasons why you might want to hide your address: it might sound too domestic, and you might not want people turning up on your doorstep! You can do this with a P.O. Box number, which starts at £60 per year and is easily set up with Royal Mail.

Alternatively, you can rent a mailbox at Mail Boxes Etc., which will give you a more tailored and personal service than a P.O. Box. Plus, you do get a nice sounding address – and a place to meet other home business owners too!

- Royal Mail
  www.royalmail.com
- Mail Boxes Etc.
  www.mbe.uk.com

Home help

Another idea is to get some help, from a call handling service, for example. They will answer your calls with your company name, text urgent messages to you and email the others, giving you a big business feel for about £50 per month. A good number of my homeworking friends use a service called Moneypenny, but there are other providers too, including Regus and My Ruby.

When holding meetings, consider hiring meeting space. Many offer serviced addresses and secretarial services too, so there could be great continuity for your clients if they only have to remember one address.

- Moneypenny
  www.moneypenny.biz
- Regus
  www.regus.co.uk
- My Ruby
  www.myruby.co.uk

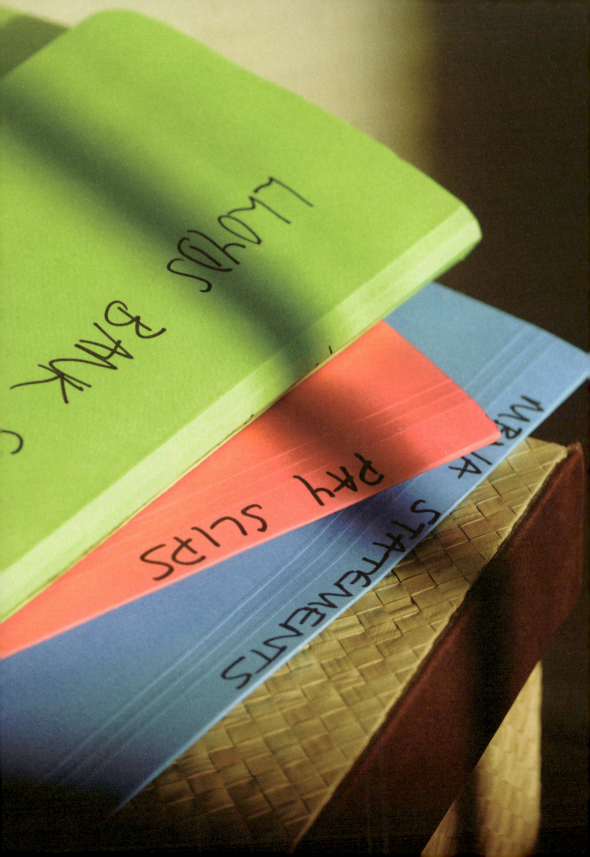

4. Managing your home business

Having made your first sale and, with the right marketing, many more, you need to be able to manage your home business so that you can keep up the momentum and grow at a comfortable pace.

The golden triangle

I use a simple triangle to help manage my home business and I try to spend an equal amount of time on each point.

1) Customer care

Look after your customers by delivering a quality product or service, on time and within budget. And remember ... the customer is always right!

I ask clients for feedback so I can keep a check on what they're thinking and changes they'd like to see.

It's good to know some personal details about your customers too. Maybe the date of their birthday, their favourite hobby or the names of their children. As you gather these details, make a quick note so you can send a birthday card on the right date, enquire after GCSE results at the right time, etc. Don't go overboard but showing that you care certainly won't harm your relationship.

2) New business

Taking care of customers means taking care of sales. Why? Because it costs less to win business from existing customers, than it does to find new ones. And if customers are happy, they'll say good things about you to new and potential customers. This is called 'word of mouth' marketing and achieving it is every home business owner's dream!

3) Admin

This is the corner of the triangle I enjoy least, but I do accept (begrudgingly) that it has to be done. It involves keeping the finances in check and the books up-to-date.

Cash is king

Keep an eye on the accounts so you can see how much money is in the bank, how much is owed and whether this covers your outgoings.

Invoices

Be on time with invoicing and keep a record of amounts outstanding. I have a simple spreadsheet with five columns labelled 'client', 'invoice amount', 'invoice number', 'date submitted' and 'date paid'.

Your invoices should be a simple document with basic details. The less cause for question on the invoice, the faster it will be paid!

Settling invoices

Settle invoices as promptly as you can. Your suppliers will be grateful and repay you with good service.

You can balance the budget with a piece of accounting software. Priced at between £50 to £100 for 'starter' versions, these packages offer sales and expense tracking, invoice templates, bank reconciliations and basic bookkeeping.

* Quickbooks
  quickbooks.intuit.co.uk
* MYOB
  www.myob.com
* Sage
  www.sage.co.uk

Receipts

Keep business-related receipts in a place where they're easy to find. I have a big wicker box that doubles as a collecting place for receipts. It's helpful that they're all in one place when it's time to do the VAT return.

Sample invoice

1. *Name of your contact*

2. *The date*

3. *An address to which the cheque should be sent or bank details in which monies should be deposited*

4. *Company registration and VAT number*

5. *Invoice number or purchase order (PO) number*

6. *Payment terms (e.g. payable within 30 days of receipt)*

7. *A brief product description or summary of services*

8. *Amount owing (inclusive or exclusive of VAT, depending on whether you're registered)*

I think it's good practice to include a cover note too, that confirms what's being invoiced and thanks the client for their custom.

Your home business

Invoice

1. Attention: Joe Smith

Managing Director

A.N. Other Home Business

321 First Street

Anytown, County AB1 2CD

2. **Date 29/01/2008**

Your home business address
123 Second Street
Anothertown, County AB2 3CD
3. **T** 01234 567 8910
F 01234 567 8911
you@youremailaddress.com
http://www.yourwebsite.com/

4. Your company registration
VAT no. 12345678910

5. PROJECT TITLE: A.N. Other Home Business website

PROJECT DESCRIPTION: Redesign of business website

INVOICE NUMBER: 01

6. TERMS: 30 days

8.

7.

Description	Amount owed
Graphic design	£1,500.00
Programming	£2,000.00
Hosting	£500.00
Total	**£4,000.00**

Please make cheque payable to Your Name and deliver to the address printed on this invoice.

Sincerely yours,

Your Name

Homeworking FAQs

As a final checklist, here are answers to the most frequently asked questions on homeworking. So you'll now know just about all you need to know on the business of starting a home business!

Q: Do I need planning permission to work from home?
A: You'll need planning permission if you answer 'yes' to any of these questions:

- Will your home business mean more traffic on your street or more people calling at your house?
- Will your home business involve any activity considered unusual for a residential area?
- Will your home no longer be used mainly as a private residence?
- Will your home business disturb your neighbours at unsociable hours or with unreasonable noise or smell?

You can see that what planners really want to know is whether you'll disturb your neighbours by having customers visiting or noisy deliveries. If this is the case, it's best to get in touch with the council, but if you'll be housing the business quietly at home, don't worry, you won't need planning permission.

- Planning Portal
  www.planningportal.gov.uk

Q: Do I need to tell the local authority I'm working from home?

A: This depends on whether you pass the planning test. If you need planning permission, you'll have to inform your local authority. If you don't, then the only benefit of telling them is that they'll charge you business rates (rather than council tax) on the part of the house being used for business purposes – not really much of an incentive! Business rates are different in each area and something that should be agreed with your local authority.

• My Business Rates
  www.mybusinessrates.gov.uk

Q: Do I need to inform my mortgage provider?

A: Yes, it's best to let them know even though it shouldn't mean any change in the mortgage repayment. If you're buying a new home in a dedicated live/work property, you'll be eligible to apply for a specialist live/work mortgage.

• Live Work Homes
  www.liveworkhomes.co.uk

Q: What about my insurance provider? Do they need to know?

A: Yes, do inform your insurance company. Tell them the equipment and stock you have at home. An upgrade from domestic to a business policy is not expensive so don't be put off in making this call. Your insurance provider is likely to recommend that you also take out public liability insurance in case anyone who comes to visit suffers an injury in or around your home office.

Q: Do I need protection for when customers and contacts come to visit?

A: Yes, carry out a health and safety check, which is easy to do by following the steps set out by the Health & Safety Executive in their Homeworking Guide.

- Health & Safety Executive
  www.hse.gov.uk

Q: How do I make sure my home 'work' doesn't take over my home 'life'?

A: Read on!

Lifestyle

5. Setting up your home office

It's not quite as straightforward as finding a spare table and chair, but working from home makes it a whole lot easier to set up an office that perfectly suits you and your home business.

Finding space

When setting up your home office, the first thing to do is find some space. And the best kind is dedicated. So, if you have a spare room, an attic or even a shed, claim it as your own and stick a sign on the door – 'my home office'.

That will help make it clear to your friends and family that when you're in your home office, you're working. And when the door's closed, it means, 'I'm busy. Please don't disturb'.

Spare room

Keeping a room as a dedicated home office also helps you know when you should be working and when you should be taking a break. Having somewhere you can close a door on can help you feel a sense of separation from your work and life, which is important. Without it, you could wind up working around the clock!

A homeworking friend, Joanna Ellis, appreciates the importance of a separate home office. "I converted a room into a working space," she says, "and it's so much better for me than camping in the lounge! Now that I've separated my home office from the rest of my home, I feel like I'm actually 'going to work'."

Other homeworkers opt to take a walk to get in the right frame of mind. Leaving via the front door and going to the side door means 'entering work' and reversing this is 'leaving work' on the way home. It's a good way of changing your mindset.

I feel the same. And, like many of my homeworking friends, I converted a spare room into a home office. Even so, my work still spills into the rest of the house. On occasion, my lounge becomes a makeshift recording studio for my video podcast, the dining table is cleared for meetings and the kitchen becomes a tea-sipping staff room for my team!

Shed

But if you don't have a spare room, why not take a walk down the garden path and into your shed? 'Shedworking' is a growing phenomenon here in the UK and has spurred an industry in garden office manufacture. But if you already have a shed, kick out the lawnmower and see how you get on!

Zheni Warner, an abstract artist from Norwich, has a dedicated studio in her garden. "When I paint I need to be alone," she says. "So we built a studio in our back garden. All I can hear is the doves on the roof – and it's wonderful."

CASE STUDY

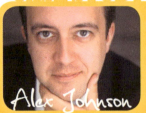

**Alex Johnson,
Shedworking**

Alex has worked as a part-time journalist from his shed since returning to the UK from Spain in 2002. Doing so, he says, means he can balance his workload with his family commitments.

"I work part-time so that I can take care of my two children," he says. "And I keep guidelines about how much time I spend with my family and on my work for clients, so that both are happy with their expectations.

"I work in a garden shed, which is being recognised – universally – as one of the healthiest working environments. It certainly is for me and for my family."

Alex is so fond of the way he works that he keeps a blog, Shedworking.co.uk, for other shedworkers as well as a quarterly magazine, The Shed, which he writes and edits from his garden office.

> *"I work in a garden shed, which is being recognised – universally – as one of the healthiest working environments."*

Kitchen table

In a purely domestic home, the kitchen is perhaps the busiest room. And a growing number of 'kitchen table tycoons' are also making it the most productive. Businesses have been born from the breakfast bar and laptops then folded away to make way for meals.

Jayne Lawton started her highly successful home business, GroBox Gardens Ltd, in the same way, and continues to run the operation from her kitchen. "I use my laptop to make phone and video conference calls to suppliers across the globe," she says. "I'm now trading worldwide – and all from my kitchen table!"

Painting and decorating

Once you've found space in the house (or outside the house) it's time to decorate and furnish your home office. And there are some tips and tricks that will have you working at full speed and in good health.

Colours and lighting

Try and find a room that has lots of natural light. If it gets too bright you can diffuse the light with blinds or muslin. And buy yourself a good task light that doesn't shine on your monitor. If you're going to paint your home office, go for light colours. They'll make the room look bigger and brighter.

Art

When it comes to hanging art in your home office, why not make your own? You don't need to be able to paint to do so. What I do is hang what I call a 'vision board', complete with photos and cuttings that represent the things I'd like to achieve with my business and in my personal life. It hangs by the door so I can see it when I come into my home office and as I turn out the lights at the end of each day.

Amanda Alexander runs her company, Corporate Mothers, from a home office that's all feng shui'd out! "It's painted a warm yellow, with a beautiful painting on one wall," she says. "There's a money plant on the windowsill and a scented candle that I light when I work late. It's very feng shui!"

TIP

Conducive colours
Soft tones of blues and greens will make a home office – and you – work particularly well.

Storage

A cluttered desk, I've always thought, is like a cluttered mind. It's no good for your home or your business, so make sure you've got good storage to keep it organised and filed away.

Here are some things to think about when buying storage:

* Buy boxes with lids and label them well
* If you have a lot of folders and boxes, consider a screen to hide them from view
* Buy a big box that can double as storage and a seat for visitors to your home office

I use a combination of storage boxes and coloured folders to keep my work for clients in order as well as my admin stuff – receipts, tax returns, bank statements, for example. I then routinely archive these to the filing cabinet that my spare room wardrobe has become!

It works well, because the wardrobe door slides shut to hide the filing cabinet. And it's mirrored too, so it makes the room look bigger.

Be careful, however, not to overcrowd your home office with storage boxes and filing cabinets. It'll make the room look small and busy – and make it harder for you to concentrate.

Furnishings

The two most important pieces of furniture for your home office are the two you'll spend most time at: your chair and your desk. So, don't scrimp on your purchases.

Buy a chair that's designed for computer use – and try it out! Sitting in an awkward position can put your body under stress, so make sure you can adjust the chair's height and angle to suit your pose. Ideally, your feet should be flat on the floor and your back straight. Getting this right will make working from home so much more comfortable!

And what about the desk?

I love the story of Jeff Bezos, founder of Amazon.com, who saved on start-up costs by using old doors as desks! If you've a bit more money, get a good, sturdy desk that can accommodate your computer, monitor, keyboard and mouse. The top of your monitor should be at eye level and the monitor itself about an arm's length away from you.

Keep it clean

Spring might be the ideal time for a big 'home office clean-out', but there are some things you can be doing all year round to keep the home office in ship-shape condition.

Get rid of those unsightly cables and invest in a wireless router. It'll liberate your Internet connection so you don't need to be plugged in to log on. Also consider getting a USB hub to connect all of your peripherals. Store it away and then connect just one cable (rather than many) to your computer.

If you're the type who likes to fiddle and fidget while you think, use that time to do some cleaning!

Throw it out!

If, like me, you keep collecting stuff, at some point you're going to have to throw some of it out (or move into a bigger house!). When you have to, be brave! And take comfort in the fact that you'll be giving it to a good home office. There are lots of websites that will match your unwanted items with people who do want them.

- Freecycle
  www.uk.freecycle.org
- Green Works
  www.green-works.co.uk

TIP

Positioning the furniture
- *Keep furniture an inch or two away from the wall*
- *Make space between your furniture*
- *Scale furniture to the size of your room. If furniture is too tall, it can make the ceiling appear lower.*

Keyboard clean
Slide sticky tape between the rows of keys on your keyboard. The adhesive side will remove dust and crumbs. It works in seconds.

Creating the right environment

You've found your space, furnished and decorated it, now you just need to add the finishing touches to create an atmosphere that will arouse your senses and leave you feeling fit and ready for work.

Sound

San Sharma, a colleague and good friend of mine, is something of a music fan. He tells me to listen to music with 'low information load' when I'm trying to concentrate. That's music with little variety and few or no lyrics.

When you need to raise your energy levels, he says, listen to something new and different. "New music introduces demands on your brain and can raise your energy levels," San says. "So when you're feeling sluggish, tune into something different, like an Internet radio station."

Reports show that people who listen to music while they work perform better than those who don't, so it's worth experimenting with sounds to find what works for you.

**Mike Rimmer,
Home based DJ**

Mike Rimmer is a music journalist and radio producer and presenter. He's been based at home since 1998, where he has his own top of the range studio. Mike says "I love homeworking because I get so much done. The only downside is that my home is too small to be able to store all the CDs I have!"

With advances in technology, Mike prepares his radio shows from his own studio, but his ultimate ambition is to broadcast live from home. This would be following in the footsteps of Mike's broadcasting hero, John Peel, who invited bands to perform at his home and live on air.

Mike's only barrier is persuading radio stations that it's possible to do so without surrendering the quality of the show. Stay tuned for developments!

Smell

Why not create your own homemade air freshener and have your home office smelling just the way you like it? A few things that I do is boil orange and lemon peel in water and let it stand, make a fresh pot of coffee and hang scented cloves in the filing cabinet. They all make for powerful aromas.

Sight

Having plants in your home office can reduce work stress, experts say. Seeing a growth in greenery can also help you feel less alone, as well as help with humidity levels, dust and productivity.

Touch

Although I don't have any pets, the neighbour's cat does visit occasionally. It's nice to feel her around my feet (although I'd be useless at feeding her!). Pets are known to reduce stress and can be an excellent source of company.

TIP

Small spaces
If you're tight on space, tempered glass or acrylic furniture appears to take up less space, so is better suited to smaller rooms. And consider buying desks and storage units on wheels so they can be pushed against the wall when not in use.

The pet debate

I asked other homeworkers what they thought about keeping pets in the home office and was surprised by the number of responses! Here are some from our Internet forum.

Liz: "I was talking to a home based client today and heard a strange squeaking noise. I suggested calling her back, thinking there was some sort of interference on the line, but she laughed and said it was her guinea pig, resting on her knee!"

Philip: "I'm not sure how impressed my clients would be to know that I was looking after their business interests while at the same time stroking my hamster. Well, I do know. Not very. Keep pets (if you really must have one) where they should be, which is nowhere near the office."

The debate continued, but the general consensus was very much that pets had their place in the home office (but beware, warned one poster, of cat prints on your keyboard – and mystery typos in your document!).

A friend to the environment

A dog might be a homeworker's best friend, but a homeworker is a keen friend of the environment too. Working from home means less time on the road and less CO_2 in the air.

But there are other things you can do to help save the planet from the comfort of your home office.

Put on a jumper!

Rather than reaching for the 'on' button to heat your entire house, why not just heat your home office (if no-one else is at home). Or put on an extra jumper to stay warm.

Be on standby

Using your computer's standby mode can conserve energy – and switching off the mobile phone charger has the same effect. Turn off the computer when you're finished for the day.

Think before you print

Cut down on printing by reading documents on screen, saving web pages etc. as web archive files, or, if you have to print, choose the double-sided option and try to re-use your scrap paper.

Recycle

Avoid buying heavily packaged goods where possible and recycle home office items like paper, batteries, print cartridges and electrical items.

- Recycle-more
  www.recycle-more.co.uk

Keep travelling to a minimum

Use teleconferencing and videoconferencing to cut down on travelling to meetings. This will save you time and money, and will help save the environment too.

- The Carbon Trust
  www.carbontrust.co.uk

CASE STUDY

Adam Constantine

Adam Constantine
Adam Constantine runs a design business from his home office in Shrewsbury – one of Shropshire's first "carbon neutral" companies.

Adam aims to offset the carbon his home business consumes. He does this by using a cooler that uses less power and by working out of an office that's built from sustainable material, which is fully recyclable.

All of his light bulbs are energy efficient and he uses public transport whenever he can. His home business uses printers who can provide eco-solutions – from using 100% recycled paper to using recyclable vegetable – based inks that don't damage the ozone.

Remember!
Staples

Ink Refills

Pens

Remember!
Eggs
Butter
Pasta

6. Balancing work and life commitments

When your home becomes your place of work, the job of blending your work and your life becomes a whole lot easier. Here are a few ground rules to help you along.

Working alone

If, in the morning, your partner leaves to work in a traditional office, whilst you stay at home, don't feel guilty or compensate by spending the day on domestic chores. Homeworking means just what it says!

Saying that, your partner will want to come back to a house that's a home, rather than your business headquarters. So it's nice to have the office closed off and the house back to a home when your loved one comes through the door.

Working with a partner

It's a different story, however, if you work at home with your partner, spouse or companion. And it's something I'm seeing a lot of – husbands and wives working and living under one roof. Does it work? It certainly seems to.

Sarah Wrixon, Pomegranate PR Ltd
Sarah runs a self-proclaimed kitchen table PR company. Except it's not exactly run from the kitchen table as this space is reserved for homework club when Sarah's girls come back from school. They work while they wait for Mum and Dad to finish for the day. That is a mum and dad who work together in the same house.

Sarah says:
"Homeworking with my husband is lovely! He works upstairs in what used to be the au pair's room. It's now a very masculine home office – with a high tech hi-fi and gadgets everywhere! And I work downstairs, with more campaign photos than boys toys!

"We meet for lunch and to walk the dog, when we talk about our businesses. The kids, we think, definitely benefit from both of us being around. And we love the flexibility it gives us. We can both go to sports day and not worry, because we'll work through the night if we need to."

**Marie Watson,
Tail-Swishing**

*Marie has found a role
for just about everyone
in her family.*

*"My husband designed
and now maintains the
website, my 18 year old
helps with advertising,
my 16 year old helps
with uploading stock,
my 14 year old helps
with descriptions and
spell-checking, my
9 year old helps find
stock to parcel, my 2
year old makes sure
Mummy takes a break
and my Mum wraps
and parcels stock
ready to take to the
Post Office."*

*Wow. That's one busy
family!*

Working with your kids

Working with your partner can be a great way to bring
you closer together, but what's the effect of homeworking
on your kids?

Well, there's good news here too. If every homeworking
mum and dad I've ever spoken with is anything to go by,
then I'd say that running a business from home means
your children get well looked after.

Being in the house not only means you can be more
attentive to your children's needs, but working around
them provides an excellent role model and a business
education too!

When I was growing up, my mum ran a restaurant and
we lived 'above the shop' so I know, first-hand, how a
home business can help keep a family together.

Nikki Spencer, freelance journalist

For more than a decade, Nikki Spencer worked as a TV reporter and journalist on a variety of shows for the BBC and Channel 4, including 'The Big Breakfast'. She then decided to go freelance and now works from a garden studio that she's nicknamed the iShed, writing articles for national newspapers and magazines including 'The Guardian', 'The Independent' and 'Junior'.

"I wanted to be able to spend more time with my children while they still wanted to spend time with me!" Nikki says. "They grow up so quickly – I didn't want to look back and feel like I'd missed out.

"I remember once, lying to my boss that my car had broken down so that I could go to my daughter's sports day. I hated feeling torn between my work and my family. When I worked in TV I often travelled for over an hour each way and was rarely home for the girls' bedtime.

"Being freelance means that I can juggle things to make sure I'm always there when needed.

"It's peaceful in my iShed. In the school holidays, the girls can have friends over and I can't hear a thing, save for the bird song and the occasional buzz of the intercom, letting me know that my eldest daughter has made lunch. You don't get that in a traditional office!"

Neighbours

As well as keeping your partner and your children happy, there's another relationship – not much further from home – that's worth keeping sweet. From experience, I'd say it's best to keep your neighbours firmly on side.

It's easy to do:

- Explain to your neighbours that you're running a business from home that shouldn't cause them any disturbance.

- Keep your promise and try to keep disruptions to a minimum. Avoid big heavy deliveries at anti-social hours and streams of client traffic clogging up the roads.

- If the business reaches a major milestone, maybe host a party for your neighbours. A friend of mine said his neighbours were more than happy to 'be on the telly' when his home business appeared on a Sky News live broadcast from his home office!

- Make friends with other homeworkers in your neighbourhood, so you can demonstrate together that the way you work is beneficial to the economy of the area and its safety, as you can keep an eye on your neighbours' houses during the day.

- If you know of a time when there'll be an unusual amount of activity in your home office, let your neighbours know in advance and perhaps send a bottle of wine to thank them for their co-operation.

Benefits to your work/life balance

Work benefits

- *The 60 second commute!*
- *Getting more done, without distractions*
- *The financial savings*
- *Being able to give your clients a personal service and a homely welcome when they visit the office*
- *Adding to the property value of your home (research carried out on my website showed that homes with offices sell for an average £25,000 more than homes without offices)*

Life benefits

- *Spending more time with friends and family. Or anything else, for that matter!*
- *Feeling happier and healthier, and enjoying the benefits this brings to your relationships*
- *Wearing what you like*
- *Dancing in the office!*
- *Being a friend to the environment so the next generation can enjoy their life too*
- *Going shopping when there are no queues*

7. Taking care of yourself

When you start and grow your business at home, you'll soon realise that you are your number one asset. And you're an asset that needs to be well taken care of.

Food

Working from home doesn't mean, as some fear, that you'll be reaching for the biscuit tin every few minutes. In fact, quite the opposite. Working in, above or next to the kitchen means you're more likely to make yourself a healthy lunch.

One thing I couldn't do without is coffee. And I know I'm not the only homeworker who enjoys a cup or two each day. But I do balance this out by drinking up to a litre of water each day. It really does seem to have a cleansing effect on both body and mind.

And then, at the end of the day, it's time for my reward. A glass of Merlot, please, or a little Sauvignon Blanc!

- 1click2cook
  www.1click2cook.com

TIP

What's on the menu?

To fuel your homeworking day, try these natural food stuffs that will have you in your best condition:

- *Fish – well known for its label of being a staple 'brain food'*
- *Oats – a source of fibre and slowly digested starch that wards off hunger*
- *Eggs – a wonder food containing Vitamin A that's good for eyesight*
- *Nuts – a source of calcium and magnesium, helping to keep your bones strong*
- *Bananas – high in tryptophan, which the body turns into serotonin (the happy chemical), so eating a banana a day helps you put a spring back in your step*

Entertaining

When you work from home, you might find that your friends and neighbours pop 'round for a chat, even if you're in the middle of work!

Of course, you will have been more productive in the rest of the day, so can afford a little time for socialising. Keep a selection of nibbles on hand to serve your home office guests.

Fitness

There are a million and one things you can do to keep fit, either in or outside of your home office.

Inside

When inside your office, why not work on a daily routine of:

- Walking up the stairs two at a time
- Chair squats – lift your butt off the seat and hover over your chair for two or three seconds. Stand up and repeat.
- Bicep curls – hold a full water bottle in your right hand and, with your abs in and spine straight, curl the bottle towards your shoulder. Repeat other side.

Outside

If you're more of an outdoorsy type, then a daily jog or gentle morning stroll could work wonders. You get exercise, fresh air and a chance to mull things over. If I ever have a big question that needs an answer, I go for a walk in the park.

I also make two trips to the gym each week, which helps to keep my mind on full alert and my body in semi-good shape!

The homeworking warm-up

According to experts in the field of ergonomics, typing is an 'athletic' event for the hands and wrists so they need to be warmed up before typing, much like legs before jogging.

Here's what I learnt from my friend and fitness instructor, Ceri Hannon.

Before typing:

- *Flex and stretch your wrists and fingers as if you're about to do a headstand. Hold this position for about 10 to 15 seconds.*
- *Make a tight fist with both of your hands and hold them for 10 to 15 seconds.*
- *Bend your wrists down, keeping your fists tightly clenched and hold for another 10 to 15 seconds.*
- *Straighten your wrists and relax your fingers. Hold this position for 5 to 10 seconds.*
- *Take frequent short breaks and simply drop your hands to your lap for just 5 to 10 seconds.*

CASE STUDY

Ingrid Blake,
The Cyber Sec

Ingrid Blake is a specimen of good health. She runs her business, The Cyber Sec, from her home and manages to keep fit too.

Ingrid was made redundant from a major UK retailer. Rather than look for another job, she saw this as the opportunity she'd been waiting for to start her own home-based business.

"I started my company, a web-based secretarial service called The Cyber Sec in April 2006 at home. Working from home has brought great benefits, one of the top ones being flexibility. I have 2 sons, who I take and collect from school and I get to watch class assemblies and take part in school activities. I can quite often be found at the kitchen table, me on my laptop and the boys doing their homework!

"I can wear what I like, eat when I like and to a certain extent, work when I like. I choose what is best for me."

Choosing what's best for Ingrid also means setting aside time for exercise.

"I have a personal trainer 3 times a week. The sessions start at 9am for an hour, which I find not only keeps me fit and healthy, but makes me feel invigorated and ready to tackle the day ahead. I think it's important to set aside some time for yourself during the working day."

Fashion

The beauty of working from home means you leave behind the daily dilemma of wondering what you should and should not wear to work. On days with no appointments, you only have yourself to look at. And, believe me, it can save you a small fortune on your wardrobe budget!

And it's certainly a myth that many home business owners work in their pyjamas. I personally feel much more productive if I wear something quite smart when I'm working and change into something more comfortable when I'm done for the day. It helps me separate the two functions of my home.

It's also nice to dress up a bit when you do head out of the home office for a meeting or event.

Get out of the office!

Working from home is a joy, but don't be afraid to admit when you start to miss human contact. It's perfectly natural and also an issue that can be resolved, without making a permanent move from your home office.

What I do is occasionally visit local coffee shops. Most of them have Wi-Fi, so I can continue with my work as normal. It's nice to have coffee that's made by someone else and it's good – every once in a while – to be around other people.

The gentle hum of chit-chat and the constant motion of passers-by can be great for your productivity, but the real advantage is being able to have this whenever you want. Working from home means you can be alone when you need to and around others when it helps. Traditional office workers don't often get that choice!

Time for a hobby

With the extra time you'll gain in working from home, why not take up a new hobby? Maybe learn a new language, enrol on a photography course or lend your hand to arts and crafts.

Antonia Chitty of ACPR says "For me, working from home is far healthier than working in an office. I can drink and eat healthily, without relying on expensive sandwich bars. I get regular breaks and exercise – running the children to school and walking through the park. I set aside one evening each week for a course for my own personal development and interest, otherwise it's easy to let every spare moment be consumed by work."

TIP

Your own home business group

Many of my website members write in to say they'd like to meet each other.

'Why not arrange a meet-up?' I say. Then you can get together with fellow home business owners to 'talk shop' and be back in the office in hours. I think these meet-ups are good for the business, mind and soul!

I use the extra time to brush up on my language skills, by listening to Japanese podcasts, whilst I do my admin. They take me right back to my time in Japan! And they're free to download. You can find a whole host of free podcasts in the iTunes Store. Or log on to lynda.com to sign up to an online training course or visit etsy.com to show off your craft talent.

- iTunes
  www.apple.com/itunes
- Lynda.com
  www.lynda.com
- Etsy
  www.etsy.com

CASE STUDY

Marni Jalif, Hospitality Store

Marni runs a website that sells catering equipment. She's a role model in getting the work/life blend just right.

"Office calls are directed to my mobile when I'm out and about," she says. "We've outsourced storage, packing and distribution to a local logistics company, leaving me time to deal with customers and meetings.

"My office is tidy and airy and I work between 9.30am and 4pm, so I have time for my family. My children have their own little jobs so they don't take things for granted!

"I find networking extremely helpful, as it keeps you fresh. It's always nice to meet like-minded people and even if you don't make a business contact you always have a nice chat and a break from the norm without feeling guilty that you're not working!

"My home office works well because I can pop into the garden for a breather and make myself a healthy, super-food juice. I think I'm doing well to balance my home and business life."

THE NUDIST ON THE LATE SHIFT

THE NUDIST ON THE LATE SHIFT

AND OTHER TR

PO BRONSON

a whole new mind

Daniel H. Pink

HOW
INFORM
TRAN

ROL

THE DREAM SOCIETY

It's not so much a 'hobby', but reading is a great way to help you relax, turn off from business, or think about things in a different way.

Here's a small selection of what's on my home bookshelf.

- *Smart Luck*, Andrew Davidson
- *The Tipping Point*, Malcolm Gladwell
- *A whole new mind,* Daniel H. Pink
- *Letter from America*, Alistair Cooke
- *The Nudist on the Late Shift*, Po Bronson

And, whilst we're at it, how about watching a few films that can teach us a thing or two about business!

- *Jerry Maguire* – great customer service, with a smattering of romance
- *Big Fish* – talent gathering and teamwork
- *Erin Brockovich* – steely determination
- *Indecent Proposal* – money can't buy everything!

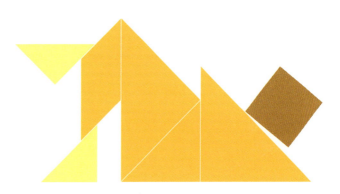

CASE STUDY

Heather Bestel

**Heather Bestel,
Founder, a little bit of me time**
*Heather Bestel was running a busy stress
management consultancy, travelling across the UK
to speak at conferences and volunteering her time to
committees and business mentoring for The Prince's
Trust. This was in the midst of running a home and trying to start a family. Yet
Heather found that the more complicated her life became, the more she craved
simplicity. So she decided to do something about it.*

*"The irony was that I was spending my working
day advising people about balancing their work and
personal life and reducing their stress, when all the
time I was adding to mine. More and more people
are choosing a simpler way of life. For some, this has
meant leaving a career, house and city behind to start
again in the country. That's exactly what I did!"*

*On 1st February 2006, Heather and her family moved into a beautiful
farmhouse four miles out of Scotland's famous Book Town, Wigtown:
"It was a dream come true. The house is perched on a hill overlooking
panoramic views of the most beautiful countryside. There is a path from our
house that leads down to the River Bladnoch, where we can sit and watch the
deer drinking and the otters playing."*

*Heather explains with a smile that their lifestyle has changed quite
dramatically. The family goes out for dinner only on special occasions and
a trip to the cinema is a big treat – to watch films a few months after they've
reached the big cities! But Heather doesn't feel as if they're missing out.*

*"We see ourselves staying here for the rest of our lives. Our only regret is that
we didn't do it sooner. We love absolutely everything about downshifting, apart
from the word itself. It sounds as though it means doing without, when actually,
we feel richer than we ever have."*

*In November 2007, Heather and husband, Peter, launched their new website
from which they sell their 10 minute relaxation CD. They are developing the site
and business together, from their dream home.*

Multitasking

You can combine a few of the activities mentioned here by multitasking. When done right, it can save you time and allow you to be more productive.

Use your head. Twice.

The trick is to combine activities that require more of your attention with those that require none. For example, for most people, doing the laundry or washing the dishes takes no thought at all. Why not use that time to think of a new marketing idea and kill two birds with one stone?

Brain and brawn

Another good example of multitasking is to incorporate exercise into your activities, combining work for the brain and the body. If you need to get together with a friend or colleague why not meet them for a jog and catch up whilst you work out?

Earn and enjoy

When you run a business from the comfort of your own home, you'll see just how much you can blend your work and your life. How you can involve the family in the business and have time left over for your hobbies and interests. It's a great way to earn a living and to enjoy living.

MarketPlace	: Ebay
Order Number	: 190938736666-926118960009
Ship Method	: Hermes Tracked
Order Date	: 2014-01-03
Email	: crazyrockchickamber@hotmail.com

Items : 1

Qty	Item	Locator
1	Spare Room Start Up: How to Start a Business from	MUL-7-UF-140-08-7
	ISBN : 1905641680	RY

RCode: |||||||||||||||||||||||||||||||||||||||||||||||||||||||||||||||||||||||||||||||||||||||

Please note:

Items are dispatched individually. If you have ordered multiple books they will

arrive in separate packages

We hope that you are completely satisfied with your purchase and ask you to leave positive feedback accordingly.

However, if you are unsatisfied with your order, please contact us by telephone or email. We wiii do whatever it takes to resolve the issue.

Mulberry House, Woods Way, Goring By Sea, West Sussex, BN12 4QY. Tel:+44(0)1903 507544
Email: ebay@worldofbooks.com | Twitter: @WorldofBooksltd | Web: www.worldofbooks.com

Technology

8. Finding the right technology

Working from home means you don't have the luxury of an IT department – or the headache! What you do have is the freedom to choose the tools that are right for you and your home business, as well as the flexibility to work when and wherever you want.

Building the right system for your home business needn't mean starting from scratch or spending oodles of money. Once your business grows you can upgrade your technology as and when funds become available. To start with, there are affordable, even free solutions that can get you up and running in no time at all. Chances are you have some of them already!

So, let's take a look at what you might already have and what you might need to buy. And we'll separate them by hardware and software.

Hardware

Hardware is the physical components of your IT system. At a basic level, it includes things like your keyboard and mouse, but can extend to include new devices and gadgets that we'll look at here and in the next chapter.

But first, let's look at the basic components of a home based IT system.

Computer

When starting out, using your home's shared computer will be just fine. You can work on it during day, when there's no-one home, and let the rest of the family use it in the evenings.

Bear in mind, however, that in the first few months of starting your home business you may find yourself working more hours than usual, trying to get it all set up.

Also, when your business grows, the data you accumulate – information on your customers, clients and contacts, including financial details – will become more and more valuable. You might then think twice about sharing your computer with the rest of the family!

For that reason, and the flexibility you'll have in deciding when and where you can work, I'd recommend looking into buying a laptop computer, if you don't have one already. There was a time when doing so was much more expensive than buying a desktop computer, but in recent years the prices have almost levelled off.

Budget laptops start at around £400, but when buying computers it's always best to buy the best that you can afford. It'll help you prepare for the future, when new software is released with new demands on your hardware; it'll help you run more programmes at once and hold more data, as your business grows; and it'll take the sting out of your purchase when prices start to drop in a few months time!

What sort of computer shall I get?

There's an ongoing debate amongst home business owners as to what's the best kind of computer to use – a Mac or a PC. Personally, I use a Windows PC, but my colleague, San, and many of the home business owners I come across use Macs and swear by them. But there are definitely advantages to both.

The advantages of a Mac

- *They're more secure than PCs. Last year, there were 114,000 viruses targeted at PCs and zero for Macs!*

- *Macs come with most of the software you need to start a home business, including powerful e-mail, calendar and address book programmes, plus website building and publishing tools. The latest Macs even include a camera built into the screens, so making video calls is easy.*

- *The Mac operating system is very stable. You'll also spend less time restarting your computer when you install new hardware or software.*

- *You can run both the Windows and Mac operating systems on one Mac. In fact, the latest version of Windows runs faster on a Mac that it does on a PC.*

- *They also look really great!*

The advantages of a PC

- *Both laptop and desktop PCs start at lower prices and better specifications than most Macs.*

- *There is more software available for PCs, especially games.*

- *More people use PCs than Macs, so there are more people to help you when you get stuck!*

- *PCs offer more control over their operating systems. You can tweak the workings of your system to suit.*

- *It's also easier (and probably cheaper) to upgrade PCs than it is most Macs.*

TIP

Burn, baby burn!
What do people mean when they say they're 'burning' a CD or DVD? Don't worry, they're not doing it any damage. 'Burning' is the process of writing to a CD or DVD. It's useful for backing up your work, making mix CDs from playlists or for sharing your home videos. You can usually only write to a CD or DVD once, so the data is usually compiled first and 'burnt' in one go.

There should be software on your Mac or PC to help you do this. If not, try a programme called Toast for your Mac or Nero for your PC.

- Toast
  www.roxio.com/
  toast
- Nero
  www.nero.com

If you've decided to buy a new computer, here are the things to look out for:

Processor
The processor is like the clock-speed of your computer. The higher the number, the faster your computer can run.

Memory
More memory (RAM) increases overall performance and enables your computer to run more programmes at once. Try and buy a computer with as much RAM as you can afford. A common frustration amongst computer users is how long it can take to launch programmes and switch between them. More RAM equals less waiting.

Hard drive
The hard drive gives you space for all your data and programmes. This can easily be expanded with a second, external hard drive, but you'll be surprised at how quickly it will fill up, especially if you're working from home and storing personal data, like music and photos, on your computer.

Display
You'll be hard pressed to find a computer that comes with a big, CRT display nowadays. Most are sold with slim, flat-screen monitors. If you don't have one already, consider upgrading. You'll save lots of space in your home office and, if you get a bigger screen with a higher resolution, you could get more work done, as you'll have more space to open programmes and documents.

Standard features
You should expect to find an optical drive, for 'burning' CDs and DVDs, and wireless connectivity, so you can get on the Internet wherever you are, with all new computer purchases.

Peripherals

Peripherals are devices that can be used with your computer but are not an integral part of it. I don't want to call them 'accessories', because some of the peripherals I use, I couldn't live without!

Multifunction printer

Even though I find myself using it less these days, with most information passed around electronically, I still think it's too early to pronounce the printer dead, especially if you use a multifunction printer like I do.

It's a real space-saver – imagine keeping a printer, scanner, photocopier and fax machine in one home office! You'd have no room to do any work! Mine sits neatly on my desk and is particularly handy when I want to e-mail sketches to my designer.

He uses his to archive printed documents. When he receives important letters, for example, he scans them into his computer and recycles the hard copy! We're both on our way to paperless home offices.

Cheryl Brighty, who makes and sells chocolates under her 'Artistry in Cocoa' brand, uses her printer for a wholly different purpose. "I design and print all our publicity at home, together with the contents labels for my chocolate boxes. Digital photography means I can update my website from home too, and having a website means having an uninterrupted shop online, if I move house."

External hard drive

I've already mentioned external hard drives. They're great for extending the storage capacity of your computer – so you can keep more data and programmes – but they're especially great for backing up your machine. This is a vital process which you should do regularly – imagine the implications if your computer crashed and wouldn't reboot. Look for ones with USB 2.0 connections or, if you're using a Mac, a FireWire connection.

They're easy to set up – you just plug them in and they show up in your operating system as another drive. You can then just drag and drop important folders or use special software that automates the process for you. Macs have this software built-in; as do the latest PCs. If not, try SuperDuper! for the Mac and True Image for the PC.

- SuperDuper!
  www.shirt-pocket.com/SuperDuper
- True Image
  www.acronis.com

Webcam

Working from home doesn't mean never seeing your colleagues again! In fact, you can switch them on and off whenever you want. If that's something that appeals to you – video chatting – consider buying a webcam. It can be fun and help you feel less alone, but also really useful when you need to have a 'face to face' meeting but can't get away. Most Macs have webcams built into their screen, for PC webcams try Logitech.

- Logitech
  www.logitech.com

Speakers

Liberated from the confines of the traditional office, working from home means you can listen to your favourite music whenever you like. No more listening through tiny earphones or to the local radio station. If you're a music fan treat yourself, and your iTunes library, to a good pair of speakers. Some are designed to be a treat for the eyes as well as the ears. My favourite set is made by a company called JBL.

• JBL Home Audio
  www.jbl.com

TIP

Docking

I use a desktop computer but my colleague uses a laptop and when he's at his home office desk he 'docks' it to an external display, keyboard and mouse and a USB hub, which keeps all of his peripherals connected, whilst keeping their cables neatly tucked away.

It's more comfortable, he says, to work that way for long periods of time, rather than at his small laptop screen and keyboard.

Network

Setting up a network used to be the work of professionals and, I suppose, in big companies they still are. But you can save yourself a small fortune by setting one up for your home. It's so much easier these days!

Your Internet service provider may have already provided you with a router – a device that allows you to share your Internet connection with other computers in your home. And many are now giving out wireless routers for free, so you can connect to the Internet all around the house – and even in the garden!

It's something Emma-Jane Batey of home business, I Can Do Better, appreciates. "We live on a farm in the middle of the beautiful Northumbrian countryside. The house has been wired for Wi-Fi, so with broadband and a speedy laptop, I could be anywhere, except I get to enjoy breathtaking views instead of office blocks."

There are two types of wireless router – one for ADSL Internet service providers, like Sky and BT, and another for cable Internet, like Virgin Media. Check with your Internet service provider to find out which is the best router for your type of connection.

I didn't get a free wireless router with my Internet service provider, but a friend recommended one that I can to you too. It's from a company called Netgear, and it actually looks quite nice too!

* Netgear
  www.netgear.co.uk

Getting connected

If you don't already have broadband, starting a home business is a good reason to get it installed. You'll need it, right from the start, during your research, while you're setting up your home business, through to when it grows and takes over the world!

Your two main options are ADSL broadband, which is offered by companies like BT, Orange and Sky and cable broadband from Virgin Media. The biggest difference is that ADSL requires a phone line while cable broadband does not.

The advantage of cable broadband is if you don't have a landline phone, and always use your mobile, you can save money by not having to pay line rental on your home phone as well as on your Internet connection. It's often faster too, but you'll need to check whether it's available in your area.

ADSL broadband is more commonplace and there are lots of companies offering it. As such, it might be easier to find a good deal. As always, read the fine print before you sign anything. Here are some things to look out for:

Price
Some broadband prices seem really cheap but often the prices advertised are for the first few months of an 18-month contract, so make sure you know what you're getting into before you sign anything.

Usage
Some broadband companies will set restrictions on the amount of data you can download in a month and sometimes even charge you extra if you go over your agreed limit. These limits rarely affect most users, but if your home business is the kind that needs to send and receive lots of information, look for deals with generous monthly download allowances. Or, better still, unlimited downloads.

Customer support
If you're installing broadband for the first time, you might need some help setting up and also, once you're up and running, knowing what to do when your connection suddenly drops. For these sorts of queries it's handy to have good customer support, so check to see what's on offer and, crucially, how much it would cost to call for help.

Keyboard and mouse

Years ago, mice used to work with a ball inside that would essentially be pushed around your desk on a mouse pad. But nowadays, there's a new technology – optical – which means no moving parts and no way for dust to get inside and interfere with the sensors. If you don't have one already, you should get one!

Again, Logitech do a nice range and also of keyboards, some of which are ergonomically designed to prevent repetitive strain injury (RSI) and wireless to cut down on clutter. Have a look around for a keyboard and mouse set and save money.

- Logitech
  www.logitech.com

CASE STUDY

Helen Dowling,
Exceptional Thinking

Helen Dowling runs a niche marketing and business planning company for small business owners. She listens to her own advice and makes the most of technology to save time and money.

"I use technology to cut down on travelling time for meetings. I now have a teleconferencing facility so I can speak to several people at once. This has saved me over £3,000 in travelling costs, which is great as it costs very little to do."

Helen has just launched e-courses on her site as a way to build the business and she's pleased with a recent upgrade to this too. "My website designer has just built me an online customer management system so I can keep track of my customers and contact them regularly with a newsletter. Because I've built a relationship with him and regularly refer clients, this was free!"

Helen certainly shows how to make the most of technology and teleconferencing!

VoIP phones

You can make serious savings on your phone bill by using a VoIP phone. VoIP stands for 'voice over Internet protocol' and it basically means making calls over the Internet rather than by using your phone line. As such, it's a much cheaper way of making calls, it's sometimes free and it's the easiest way to set up a second line.

TIP

VoIP
Find out more about VoIP on page 142.

The VoIP phone I use is made by a company called IPEVO who make handsets in black or white to go with your Mac or PC.

- IPEVO
  www.ipevo.com

Software

Software is the programmes and operating system that are used by your computer. Again, you'll be using many of them already, in your everyday life, so there's no need to splash out when setting up your home business. Once it grows you can upgrade to more advanced versions.

To start, here are the basics.

Productivity
Office software

By far, the industry standard in office software, for both Mac and PC computers, is Microsoft Office, which includes a word processor, presentation and spreadsheet programmes. But it's also quite expensive. Unless you already own it you might find it hard to justify the price tag when starting your home business. If you're trying to bootstrap, try this free alternative.

- OpenOffice.org
  www.openoffice.org

It's called OpenOffice.org and does pretty much everything that Microsoft Office can do, plus it can open and save Microsoft Office files too. It does take some getting used to, but the support is pretty good. It's worth a try!

Team software

If you'll be working with other people, you might consider project management software that keeps everyone in touch with what's going on.

I use a tool called Basecamp. Not only can my team share ideas and updates on this programme but I can invite clients to view specific projects too.

- Basecamp
  www.basecamphq.com

Personal

Along with most of my homeworking friends, I use technology in my personal affairs to free up time that can be spent on the business. I do my banking online, the same with shopping and I'm turning more and more to online postal services too.

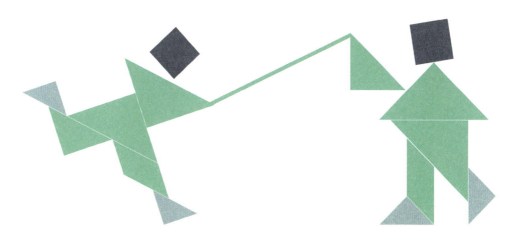

The Internet

The Internet consists of more than just the pages you surf on the web. It includes e-mail, instant messaging and VoIP. It is a suite of information and communication systems and I haven't yet met a home business owner who isn't a fan of this piece of technology! The Internet is used for research, finding partners, sourcing supplies and, of course, marketing and selling your own products and services.

As Victoria Griffiths of The FunkiJunk Jewellery Company says: "Conducting most of my business over the Internet means I don't spend hours of my day on the phone, which can disturb my young children. If I have an order to put through, I save it until the evening and pop it through when they've gone to bed. We're all winners that way."

Here are the programmes you'll need to take advantage of the Internet's many features for your home business.

Web browser

All computers come with web browsers pre-installed. It's the programme that allows you to see web pages on the Internet. PCs typically use a browser called Internet Explorer and Macs, a programme called Safari.

Both do a good job, but there's a browser I use that I think is better. It's called Firefox and it's made by a community of programmers, rather than a single company. It's faster, more secure and customisable, so you can add features that will help you do your work and manage your lifestyle. These include features to control your music (without having to switch programmes), comparison shop and even change the way your browser looks.

It's a free, small download that won't take up much memory and it works on Macs and PCs.

- Firefox
  www.getfirefox.com

CASE STUDY

Bill Morrow and Lois Cook, Angels Den

Angels Den was borne out of the background of its two founders.

Bill Morrow was an accountant and former investment banker who had worked with "blue chip" brands including Virgin and Kleinwort Benson, and Lois Cook spent many years in senior management with a Japanese multinational before moving on to help small businesses.

"Lois thought it impossible to find funding; I thought it impossible to find companies to invest in ... Angels Den was borne out of the desire to prove each other wrong. Luckily, we were both right!

"Those with money were finding it difficult to find things to invest in and companies were finding it hard to find money or people who believed in them! Angels Den puts the two together for £499, with no back-end or success fees."

Angels Den does more than that. This home-based business is revolutionizing the world of angel investment and start-up funding by transferring the process online.

Not only do Bill and Lois utilise technology as a platform for their business, they also make the most of it to run the business.

"Lois and I work from home ourselves, indeed we run the entire company using an army of home-workers.

"Our 2 brilliant admin people work flexibly. Michelle works mornings having dropped the kids off at school and Juliet who is studying for her Msc in Business Studies picks up the reins after lectures, when Michelle's kids come back from school. Our IT director works from home and co-ordinates our programmers, who programme all day long, from their sheds, in the snows of Finland."

And what do you think about TV show, 'Dragons' Den', Bill?

"Dragons' Den has been a double-edged sword for us. It has brought Angel funding to the public's attention but it's convinced our audience that you'll be ridiculed and torn apart by Dragons when you are looking for funding. The truth could not be further away. Angels are praying that you will give them 'the right answers', as they are desperate to invest."

E-mail

Again, computers come with e-mail software pre-installed. On PCs the software is called Outlook Express (or on newer PCs Windows Mail) and on Macs it's just called Mail.

If you've got Microsoft Office you might use Outlook or Entourage, as it's called in the Mac version, which is like Outlook Express's big sister. It includes calendar and address book features, but is only available if you buy Microsoft's Office suite of programmes.

An alternative is provided by the people who make Firefox. It's called Thunderbird and can do pretty much everything that Outlook can. It's fast, secure and, like Firefox, customisable. You can even use it with web-based mail, like Gmail or Hotmail, so that you can read and write your e-mail at your home office desk or in an Internet café.

Regardless of your writing and reading location, make the most of the email marketing opportunity every time you click 'send'. Include a professional email signature or sign-off that has your basic contact details (name, company, postal address, telephone, etc.) and also maybe mention any seasonal or product offers.

- Thunderbird
  www.getthunderbird.com

POP mail vs. web mail

E-mail that you usually use in a programme like Outlook or Apple's Mail is called POP mail and it works by downloading messages from a server onto your computer. The disadvantage is that once you've downloaded your messages you can only read them on your home office computer, which isn't a problem to most, but if you're out and about, in an Internet café or wanting to find an old e-mail on another computer or mobile phone, for example, you won't be able to.

Web mail is accessed through a web browser, like Firefox, and keeps your e-mail on the server, so you can read and write e-mail wherever you are. It's often provided for free through services like Microsoft's Hotmail or Google's Gmail, but is perhaps less professional sounding than POP mail, which can be addressed at your domain, for example emma@enterprisenation. com. My Hotmail address is enterprisenation@hotmail. co.uk, which doesn't look quite as good!

But there is a solution that Google provides. It's called Google Apps and allows you to use all of its web-based features, like e-mail, calendar and instant messaging at your own address. It's especially good for small businesses and organisations and it's free! You just need to own your own domain, like I do: www. enterprisenation.com

*   Google Apps
    www.google.com/a

TIP

Staying out of the Inbox
E-mails can have a habit of taking over your day. To be ultra productive, why not spend a couple of mornings out of your Inbox. Turn off the email programme and work without interruption!

Instant messaging and VoIP

A great way to stay in touch with friends and colleagues is by instant messaging (IM), which allows you to exchange typed messages over the Internet in real-time. So it's not like e-mail, where there's typically a delay in the response. Instant messaging is more like chatting. And it's a great way to instil some office-like atmosphere in your home office, with the added advantage that you can turn it off!

Charlie Dalton of garden office manufacturer, Smart Garden Offices, uses instant messaging and chat facilities to keep himself and his clients engaged. "In my six years of working from home, I've never felt isolated or separated from the rest of the world. How could I? Broadband brings e-mail, radio, 24 hour news-streams and I also use MSN messaging with suppliers as well as encouraging customers to use the chat facility on my website too."

Lots of instant messaging programmes also allow you to make video and voice calls. The programme I use best integrates text, voice and video chat and is called Skype.

It allows me to make free calls to other Skype users and to landline or mobile phones for a small fee, which is deducted from pay-as-you-go style 'Skype credit'.

You can even assign a landline-sounding phone number to your Skype account, so you can receive calls at your computer, using a VoIP handset (see page 131), or divert calls to your mobile when you're out and about.

It's worth trying it out before you spend money installing a second line.

- Skype
  www.skype.com

Support

If you're in need of help with anything from hardware set-up to software installation, then call in the help of a local IT expert. You may know a neighbour who's a dab hand at technology or another option is to check out one of a growing number of companies who send a 'geek' direct to your door.

- Geeks-on-Wheels
  www.geeks-on-wheels.com
- The TechGuys
  www.thetechguys.com
- The Geek Squad
  www.geeksquad.co.uk

A bootstrapper's software shopping list

Web browser: Firefox = £0
E-mail client: Thunderbird = £0
IM and web chat: Skype = £0
Office apps: OpenOffice.org = £0

9. Working away from home

Now that you've found the right technology for your home office – hardware and software – it's time to take it outside! If you ever get tired of your four walls, it's good to know that it's possible to work elsewhere. Here's how to, away from your home office.

New technology means it's possible to work wherever you want. You've already decided that you want to work for yourself and away from the traditional office, but now – with a few simple tips and tricks – you can enjoy unprecedented flexibility, and work almost anywhere, from your local coffee shop to the public park.

With your computer

If you already have a fairly up-to-date laptop computer, you have all you really need to work away from home. Most can pick up wireless Internet access from receivers already built-in.

But if you have a slightly older laptop you can buy a small adaptor which you plug into a spare USB port. Affordable options are available from a company called Belkin, who provide pretty clear instructions to help you get started.

- Belkin
  www.belkin.com/uk

CASE STUDY

Pat Oxley, 17 Burgate

17 Burgate is a boutique bed and breakfast in the market town of Pickering, midway between York and the coast. This home business is run by Pat Oxley and her husband. The couple use technology that gives them the freedom to travel, knowing they can keep in touch with the business wherever they are.

"Our website is our window to the world and we're constantly developing it. We're about to launch a blog and message boards so we can convey the 'style' of the business."

The Oxley's have also introduced a 'virtual tour' on their site and they make full use of the Internet to track industry information, from new laws and regulations, to competitors' details.

"We keep in touch with the business by using call divert to our mobile phones and computer access. This allows us to take enquiries wherever we are. Our best to date is whilst having a pre-dinner drink in the Moulin Rouge!"

Accessing Wi-Fi hotspots

Nowadays, if you use your laptop computer in a public place, like a coffee shop, a library, or even some public parks, you can connect to a Wi-Fi hotspot. These are wireless Internet connections that allow you to surf the web, check your e-mail and instant message when you're away from your home office.

Unless you've a kindly local council, who'll provide Wi-Fi hotspots free of charge, the chances are the hotspots you'll come across will cost you something. They usually charge for an hour's access, for 24 hours or for a month at a time and prices do vary. But at the time of writing the three main providers of wireless Internet access are BT, a company called The Cloud and T-Mobile.

- BT Openzone
  www.btopenzone.com
- The Cloud
  www.thecloud.net
- T-Mobile HotSpot
  www.t-mobile.co.uk

TIP

Free hotspots

Wi-Fi hotspots are usually free of charge in public libraries, where you'll have to be a member, or – and here's a good tip – in independent coffee shops, where owners encourage you to use their hotspots to boost sales of their goods. Coffee shop chains, like Starbucks and Costa, usually have deals with third party providers, like The Cloud and T-Mobile, which can be quite expensive.
If you can't see a sign in the window, just ask your local coffee shop owner. And if they don't have Wi-Fi, and if enough people ask, they might just get it installed!

- myHotspots
  myhotspots.co.uk

With your mobile phone

You have probably heard of the Blackberry (or, as they're referred to by their addicts, the 'Crackberry'!). They're one of the most popular devices for working away from the home office.

They allow you to surf the web, check your e-mail and edit some office documents, but they tend to be more popular with bigger businesses, who can take advantage of sophisticated features that require special Blackberry servers.

Amanda Gummer who runs Fundamentals invested in a basic PDA (Personal Digital Assistant) so she can "make use of dead time, such as sitting outside the ballet class, by checking e-mails or making a call".

If you just want to send and receive e-mail whilst out and about, buy a PDA or check with your mobile phone provider to see how it's possible.

If you use web mail, from Google for example, or Yahoo!, it's easy. Just visit their homepage on your mobile phone's web browser, if it has one, and follow the instructions.

- Yahoo! Mobile
  uk.mobile.yahoo.com
- Google Mobile
  www.google.com/mobile

At Internet cafés

If you don't fancy lugging your laptop around with you or peering at the small screen of your mobile phone, you can manage some of the day-to-day responsibilities of your home business, like e-mail, for example, from an Internet café.

If you're on holiday you'll find plenty of them around, and it's a good way of checking in on your home business without having to check out of your hotel. Most have 'business centres' with Internet connected PCs, so if you are planning a holiday remember to check your options with the hotel before you book.

If you use web based e-mail you can send and receive messages just like you would at home. If you use POP mail check with your provider that you can access new mail, before it's downloaded to your home computer, from another location. Some provide web interfaces for that reason, but they usually only show new e-mail since you last checked for messages.

Mel Henson of copywriting business, Words That Sell, knows all about working when on the move. She's switched from an ISP to Google Mail so she can access emails anywhere.

❝ Now I can go away for a few days and still give my clients a seamless service, either by visiting web cafés or using my laptop at a Wi-Fi hotspot. Another big timesaver was learning the shortcuts for Word commands, which saves me about 40 minutes a week! ❞

Everything from anywhere

If you already use web mail, you'll be used to the idea of your messages and contacts being available from any computer connected to the Internet. So, how about running your entire home business from any computer anywhere?

Web applications are programmes that are run online rather than on your computer alone. You run them through your web browser and all the data is stored on the Internet so, in effect, you can use them and your information from pretty much any computer anywhere!

The best example is provided by Google, whose Google Apps offering includes e-mail, instant messaging, a calendar, word processor, spreadsheet and presentation software, as well as a website builder.

All the work you do is stored on the Internet so you can log in and out from anywhere and see the same information. Also, if your computer crashes or you buy a new system you won't lose any data or have to re-install it on a new machine.

Google Apps is free to use and easy to set up.

• Google Apps
www.google.com/a

10. Building a home on the web

Your website is your window to the world and your home on the web. It can be used as a powerful marketing tool and a way to make money. Having the right technology and knowledge allows you to build, develop and maintain your site. And you can do it all in-house.

If we skip back to the beginning of this book, when we were thinking about starting a home business, we return to the 'name game' – the part of our planning where we think about a name for our home business.

I've been through it many times! And each time a factor has come into my decision making. And that is whether or not my proposed business name is available as a domain.

Choosing a domain

What is a domain? A domain makes up a part of your website and e-mail address. So, for example, the domain name I own is enterprisenation.com. My website address is www.enterprisenation.com and my e-mail address is emma@enterprisenation.com. Both use the enterprisenation.com domain name.

A domain isn't only your address on the web it's also a big part of your brand on the Internet. So, you must think carefully when choosing one – although your options will be increasingly limited, since so many combinations have already been snapped up.

There are domain registration companies whose websites allow you to check for available domain names and often suggest available alternatives. Here are three that I've come across.

- 1&1 Internet Ltd.
  www.1and1.co.uk
- 123-reg
  www.123-reg.co.uk
- Easily.co.uk
  www.easily.co.uk

TIP

Pick a domain
Pick a domain name that is easy to spell and memorable. This is particularly important if you're selling goods online, as opposed to building a web presence for your business.

Look for an available '.com' domain name first and then a '.co.uk'.

Avoid numbers, dashes or any special characters that you may have to explain over the phone.

Sorting out hosting

Registering a domain name doesn't give you a website, just an address for it (and an e-mail address). Think of it like reserving a car parking space. You've got the space, now you need to buy the car!

A hosting company will sort you out with the web space to host your website. This is measured in megabytes and gigabytes, just like the information on your computer. You upload the files that make up a website – pictures and pages – to this space, so that the rest of the world can see them. With a domain name and web space, potential customers should be able to type your website address into their browser and find out all about your home business.

Finding a hosting company shouldn't be hard. Most domain registration companies offer web space as a package and vice versa. There are some links on the previous page.

TIP

How much web space will I need?
Basic hosting packages offer about 250 MB of web space, but anything over 1 or 2 GB is more sensible and it will also allow you to handle more traffic on your website as it grows more popular.

Designing your website

Most hosting companies will provide some sort of web builder tool that will help you build a website without any sort of technical know-how. You just have to follow the on-screen instructions to get started.

But using such a tool can leave your website looking generic and lacking in personality and charisma. It's not a bad way to get started, but remember first impressions mean everything on the web.

Your website is sometimes the first thing potential customers will see of your home business – and they'll make their judgement in seconds! So, if you're serious about your home business, consider hiring an affordable and professional web designer, who can talk you through your ideas and how best to translate them into something visual and accessible on the web.

Corinne Young runs Ecoteriors from her home and used the art of barter to get herself a lovely looking website.

"I'm by no means a computer expert but I do realise the importance of having a website, so I set up a basic site with help from my daughter and a close friend. It's about to be updated by a designer I met at a networking event. As I had a very tight budget I negotiated with her and we've agreed a deal where I'll create artwork and soft furnishings for her home, to the same value as her services for updating the site."

Before hiring a designer, however, have a think about what you'd like your website to do for your home business. The easiest way to start is to think of your website as a brochure, but remember to include the following pages, at least.

Pages to include
- About us
- News
- Products or services
- FAQs (Frequently Asked Questions)
- Contact us

Blogging

You've probably heard of blogging. It's a website or part of a website that's regularly updated by an individual or a group of 'bloggers'. There are blogs on any number of topics and the fact that anyone can start blogging makes the medium diverse and exciting.

It's also a great way to market your home business. Search engines love blogs and the more you write the higher up the search engine ranks your website will go. Also, if you write regularly, you'll develop a loyal readership and a neat way to communicate your news with existing and potential customers. Readers can also add their comments to your entries if you allow them and you can use your blog to answer questions and establish yourself as an expert in your field.

It's free and easy to get started. Try one of the services below and link to it from your main website. It may get so popular that it becomes your main website!

- Blogger
  www.blogger.com
- TypePad
  www.typepad.com
- WordPress
  www.wordpress.com

Making money from your website

If you want to sell products on your website the easiest way to get started is with a service called PayPal. It will process credit card and other payment methods in exchange for a small commission. It's free to get an account and pretty easy to set up. If you're not sure about installing it on your website there's a way of charging customers via e-mail, by including a special link that PayPal provides.

- PayPal
  www.paypal.co.uk

eBay

Did you know that the number of people in the UK with a full time or hobby eBay business has increased by a whopping 160% over the past two years?

There are now more than 178,000 people making money from eBay and from the comfort of their own home. You could be one of them!

eBay itself started as a home-based business and has grown to become the largest shopping mall on the web. The best way to understand how eBay works, before starting to sell your products through it, is to buy a few items yourself.

Follow these five simple steps to get started on eBay and buy your first item.

Doing so will help you better understand the process of a potential customer and the way in which you handle payment and contact with your own customer.

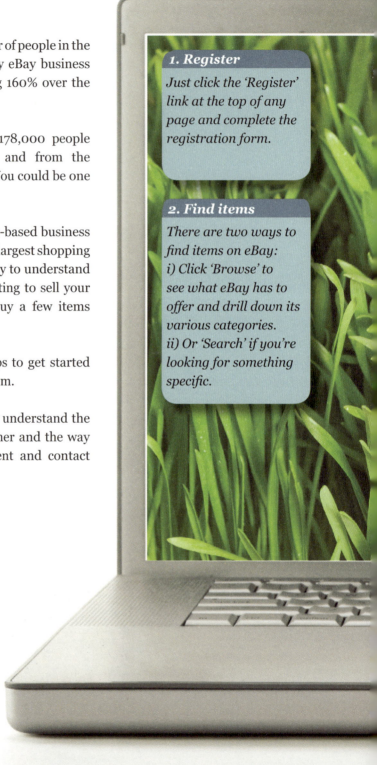

1. Register
Just click the 'Register' link at the top of any page and complete the registration form.

2. Find items
There are two ways to find items on eBay:
i) Click 'Browse' to see what eBay has to offer and drill down its various categories.
ii) Or 'Search' if you're looking for something specific.

3. Review the item and the seller

This is the really important bit. Make sure you know what you are buying and who is selling it.

4. Place a bid or buy instantly

Once you've found the item you want to buy, decide the maximum you're willing to pay and how you'd like to buy it.

Place a bid for the highest price you're prepared to pay for the item and eBay will bid on your behalf as much as is needed for you to remain the highest bidder.

Or, if you see 'Buy It Now' beside the listing you can buy the item instantly at the price stated by the seller without bidding.

5. Paying for your item

After you've won or purchased the item, it's a good idea to email the seller, and check their listing or email invoice to find out what the preferred payment method is and where you should send payment.

They'll only send the item once they've received payment. So don't delay!

CASE STUDY

John Williams
Business coach & founder, Freestyle Success

When John Williams left his last full-time role, he made a personal resolution:
"I never want another job for the rest of my life."
And so far, he's stuck to it!

With a background that included distinguished roles, from senior managing consultant at Deloitte, to special effects software developer, John didn't think there was anything intrinsically wrong with the "job" – he just felt that a fixed position with a company could no longer cater to all his passions and interests.

He now happily boasts about his "Portfolio career". A career that includes consulting on future technology, careers and business coaching and a number of creative projects, from freelance writing, producing radio jingles and performing stand-up comedy!

John's coaching business is called Freestyle Success and he works with people who want to create what he calls a "Freestyle Career" – one that "engages your creativity, pays you what you're worth, and is structured to give you time to live". His company strapline is "do what you love and make it pay".

John is also a firm follower of technology, believing it to be the foundation of a freestyle career. Creating an email database is just one of the technology tools he promotes to his clients:

"Most freelancers fail to understand the value of building an email database. Imagine that you have encouraged people on your website to give their email address and that at every event you collect more addresses.

"Now when you have a new product to sell or a workshop you want to fill you can email your list of contacts and immediately sell some of those spaces or products. If you have 200 emails, you might fill a couple of spaces on a workshop straight away. If you have 2,000, you might fill the whole workshop. Start collecting emails – with permission – now."

Attracting visitors to your site

Now you have your home on the web, you'll be eager for people to pay you a visit. Promote your website by following the marketing tips offered in chapter 3 and also practice some 'Search Engine Optimisation'.

Search Engine Optimisation

Search Engine Optimisation, commonly referred to as 'SEO', is the process by which you can improve rankings for your website in the top search engines such as Google, i.e. getting your site onto the first few pages of results rather than page 75!

Google is a search engine that uses software known as "spiders" to crawl the web on a regular basis and find sites to add to their index. There are steps you can take to make it easier for the spiders to find and add your site.

Start with the homepage

Provide high-quality, text-based content on your pages – especially your homepage. If your homepage has useful information and good quality, relevant text, it's more likely to be picked up by the spiders.

Beyond the homepage, write pages that clearly describe your topic/service/product. Think about the words users would type to find your pages and include them on the site.

Be well connected

Improve the rank of your site by increasing the number of other high-quality sites that link to your pages; these are referred to as 'inbound links'. For example, if you're running a competition, go to sites that promote competitions and add yours.

TIP

Add URL
To get started with your in-house search engine optimising, visit the Google 'Add URL' page and submit your details.

- *Google Add URL*
  www.google.com/ addurl

Tagging

A webpage's title, referred to as a 'Title Tag', is part of the SEO mix and can make a difference to your search rankings. It is also the text that appears in the top of the browser window.

Include in your title tag the main key phrase you'd like the search engines to associate with your webpage and keep it to 60-90 characters in length. Duncan Green of Moo Marketing is an SEO expert and explains "the title tag on the homepage for Moo Marketing reads: 'Moo Marketing – Search Engine Marketing – PPC Management - Search Engine Optimisation', as you can see the title element is 85 characters long, contains three key phrases and identifies the subject of the webpage."

Networking online

You can also become known across the web by networking online; in business forums such as LinkedIn, in chat groups that cater to your specific sector/trade/skill and on social media sites such as Facebook.

One site you certainly shouldn't forget to bookmark ... is mine! Visit www.enterprisenation.com and you'll meet me, all the people mentioned in this book and thousands more homeworking friends. The site brings you online content plus a fortnightly e-news and video show. It's all you need to turn your business dream into reality.

- Linked In
  www.linkedin.com
- Facebook
  www.facebook.com
- Enterprise Nation
  www.enterprisenation.com

In this chapter I've shown you how to buy the right hardware and software for your new home business, offered the basics of getting connected to broadband and mentioned some nifty gadgets and accessories that will make work so much more enjoyable - and productive!

You've also now got a guide to building your own website and making money online as well as advice on working away from your home office.

Now all you need do is sign up for the free Enterprise Nation e-news so you can receive helpful and handy tips, delivered direct to your inbox, every 2 weeks.

Sign up to the e-news online at
www.enterprisenation.com
and use technology to keep in touch!

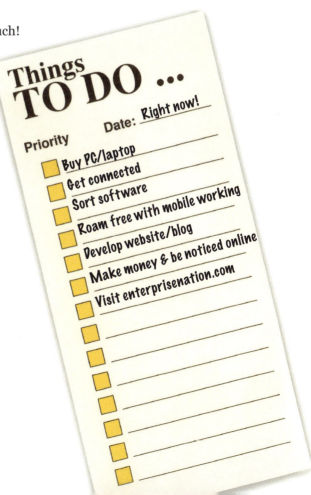

Next steps

I hope this book has provided you with all the information and inspiration you need to start your own business from home.

Over the past two years I've spoken to hundreds of home business owners and not one of them regrets the decision to become their own boss. Comments such as "I wish I'd done this years ago" and "life has never been better" are typical.

Can you imagine getting paid for doing something you enjoy, in a comfortable environment, whilst still having time left over for family and friends? There's no wonder so many home business owners say they should have started earlier!

So, with the right technology at your fingertips, all the help you need in these pages and www.enterprisenation.com as a free resource to guide you, it's time to make a start. A Spare Room Start Up!

I wish you every success and can guarantee that you'll never look back.

Happy Homeworking!
Emma Jones
emma@enterprisenation.com

Emma Jones

Emma Jones
Enterprise Nation

Emma Jones is Founder and Editor of Enterprise Nation, the home business website. She has successfully started two businesses from home offices in London, Manchester and rural Shropshire.

Following a career with an international accountancy firm, Emma started her first home-based business at the age of 27 and successfully sold it just 15 months after launch.

Spotting a gap in the market to provide information and inspiration to homeworkers, Emma launched Enterprise Nation (www.enterprisenation.com), the home business website, in January 2006.

The website is a free resource for people starting and growing a business at home and has a readership of more than 390,000 people. Visitors to the site enjoy features of successful home business owners, top tips, homeworking news stories and start-up ideas. As well as site content, there is also a free fortnightly e-newsletter and active forum.

As well as developing the website, Emma advises government agencies on how they can best encourage and support home business and her views on the subject have been quoted across the national media and in an annual Home Business Report.

Now that she's written this book, she's working on her second edition which will be all about 'how to grow your business from home' – watch this space!

Glossary

5pm 'til 9am economy
The business generated by people working on their home business during evenings and weekends.

Blog
A website, or part of a website, that's regularly updated by an individual or a group of 'bloggers'. Blogs often commentate on either life in general or one specific area, such as business, news, or politics. Readers can also add their comments to your entries if you allow them to.

Companies House
The official UK government register of UK companies. www.companieshouse.gov.uk

Domain
The name of your website, e.g. www.enterprisenation.com.

Franchise
A license permitting someone to sell a product or service under an existing trademark or trade name, for example, Avon, McDonald's, Virgin Vie.

HMRC – HM Revenue & Customs
The government department responsible for collecting the bulk of tax revenue, as well as paying some tax credits and benefits in the UK. www.hmrc.gov.uk

Hosting
A service provided by various companies which allow you to create and manage a website. This is frequently offered by ISPs, and various levels of service are available.

IMOFF
The fundamentals you need to include in a business plan: Idea, Market, Operations, Financials & Friends.

Instant messaging
The exchange of typed messages over the Internet in real-time.

ISP – Internet Service Provider
A company which provides access to the internet.

IP – Intellectual property
The legal rights of an owner of an idea, invention, brand, etc. which can be registered and therefore protected by law from being copied. Intellectual property laws include copyright, patents and trademarks.

Limited company
A company that exists in its own right, with separate finances to its owners. It is owned by shareholders, which can either be individual people or companies.

Local rate number
A phone number that you buy which then redirects to your existing phone number. The benefit is to give your business a 'national' feel. A local rate number starts '0845' and has low call charges.

National rate number
A phone number that you buy which then redirects to your existing phone number. The benefit is to give your business a 'national' feel. A national rate number starts '0870' and has high call charges.

Partnership
A company status whereby the business has two or more owners. The risk, reward and workload are shared, but so are the profits.

PayPal
An electronic way to send and receive payments. Payment can be made from funds in your PayPal account or by other payment methods, such as credit card, debit card or bank account transfer.

Podcast
An audio or video file which is available via the Internet.

POP mail
E-mail that is downloaded from the server to your computer. In contrast to web mail, which remains on the server and can be accessed from any computer.

RAM – Random Access Memory
The amount of memory your computer has.

SEO – Search Engine Optimisation
The process by which you can improve rankings for your website in the top search engines such as Google.

Sole trader
A company status whereby the business has only one owner and employee. The owner gets to keep all the profits but is also personally liable for any company debt.

SWOT analysis
An evaluation of a business in the following areas: Strengths, Weaknesses, Opportunities, Threats.

Title tag
The main phrase you'd like the search engines to associate with your webpage, which will also appear as the text in the top of the browser window.

URL – Uniform Resource Locator
Tech-speak for a website address.

USP – Unique Selling Point
The aspect(s) of your business that set it apart from the competition. USPs can be either tangible or perceived.

VAT – Value Added Tax
An indirect tax levied on goods and services in the UK. A company or trader registered for VAT pays suppliers VAT in addition to the cost of goods or services purchased. VAT is added to the sales cost of their product when invoicing customers.

VoIP – Voice over Internet Protocol
A way of using the Internet to make and receive calls rather than using a traditional phone line, for example using your broadband internet connection. It's a very cost-effective way of making calls and an easy way to set up a second phone line.

Web mail

E-mail that remains on the server and can be accessed from any computer via a web browser, e.g. Google Mail, Hotmail.

Wi-Fi

A wireless connection, which can either be an Internet one or from one device to another. Publicly available Wi-Fi is called a 'Wi-Fi Hotspot'.

Useful links

1&1 Internet Ltd.
Domain registration and website hosting
www.1and1.co.uk

123-reg
Domain registration and website hosting
www.123-reg.co.uk

1click2cook
Weekly recipes
www.1click2cook.com

Angels Den
Angel investing
www.angelsden.com

Basecamp
Project management tool
www.basecamphq.com

Belkin
Electrical products
www.belkin.com/uk

Blogger
Blogging tool
www.blogger.com

Blue Square Offices
Call handling
www.bluesquareoffices.com

BT Openzone
Wi-Fi Hotspots
www.btopenzone.com

Business Link
Government-backed business support network
www.businesslink.gov.uk

Carbon Trust, The
CO2 footprint advice
www.carbontrust.co.uk

Cloud, The
Wi-Fi Hotspots
www.thecloud.net

Companies House
Company registration
www.companieshouse.gov.uk

Easily.co.uk
Domain registration and website hosting
www.easily.co.uk

eBay
Online auction-based website
www.ebay.co.uk

Enterprise Nation
A free resource to help you start and grow your business from home
www.enterprisenation.com

Etsy
Online arts & crafts shop
www.etsy.com

Facebook
Social/business networking site
www.facebook.com

Firefox
Web browser
www.getfirefox.com

Freecycle
Give away unwanted stuff to people in your area
www.uk.freecycle.org

Geek Squad, The
IT support
www.geeksquad.co.uk

Geeks-on-Wheels
IT support
www.geeks-on-wheels.com

Gmail (Google Mail)
Web-based email
www.gmail.com

Google Add URL
Site optimisation tool
www.google.com/addurl

Google Apps
Software application
www.google.com/a

Google Mobile
Software application
www.google.com/mobile

Green Works
Redistribute second-hand office furniture
www.green-works.co.uk

Health & Safety Executive
Responsible for health and safety regulation in Great Britain
www.hse.gov.uk

HM Revenue & Customs
UK tax collection agency
www.hmrc.gov.uk

Hotmail
Web-based email
www.hotmail.co.uk

Institute of Chartered Accountants in England & Wales
Accountancy body
www.icaew.co.uk

IPEVO
Handset producer
www.ipevo.com

iStockphoto
Stock photography shop
www.istockphoto.com

iTunes
Music store
www.apple.com/itunes

J4b Grants
Information on available business funding
www.j4bgrants.co.uk

JBL Home Audio
Speaker manufacturer
www.jbl.com

UK Intellectual Property Office
Grant IP rights in the UK
www.ipo.gov.uk

Linked In
Business networking
www.linkedin.com

Live Work Homes
Property search site for homes you can also work from
www.liveworkhomes.co.uk

Logitech
Webcam producer
www.logitech.com

Lynda.com
Online training
www.lynda.com

Mail Boxes Etc.
Rentable mailbox service
www.mbe.uk.com

Moneypenny
Call handling
www.moneypenny.biz

My Business Rates
Business rates site run by the government
www.mybusinessrates.gov.uk

MyHotspots
Wi-Fi Hotspot locator
www.myhotspots.co.uk

My Ruby
Call handling
www.myruby.co.uk

MYOB
Accounting software
www.myob.com

Nero
Data back-up
www.nero.com

Netgear
Wireless router
www.netgear.co.uk

OpenOffice.org
Software application
www.openoffice.org

PayPal
Electronic payment system
www.paypal.co.uk

Planning Portal
Planning permission and building regulations
www.planningportal.gov.uk

Printing.com
Printing and design
www.printing.com

Quickbooks
Accounting software
http://quickbooks.intuit.co.uk

Recycle-more
Recycling advice
www.recycle-more.co.uk

Regus
Serviced offices
www.regus.co.uk

Royal Mail
Postal service
www.royalmail.com

Sage
Accounting software
www.sage.co.uk

Shedworking
A blog for and about Shedworking
www.shedworking.co.uk

Skype
Voice over Internet Protocol and instant messaging tool
www.skype.com

SuperDuper!
Data storage
www.shirt-pocket.com/SuperDuper

T-Mobile HotSpot
Wi-Fi Hotspots
www.t-mobile.co.uk

TechGuys, The
IT support
www.thetechguys.com

Thunderbird
Email application
www.getthunderbird.com

Toast
Data back-up
www.roxio.com/toast

True Image
Data storage
www.acronis.com

TypePad
Blogging software application
www.typepad.com

WordPress
Blogging software
www.wordpress.com

Yahoo! Mobile
Mobile email application
http://uk.mobile.yahoo.com

Profiled home businesses

17 Burgate	*www.17burgate.co.uk*
ACPR	*www.acpr.co.uk*
Adam Constantine Design	*www.adamconstantine.co.uk*
A little bit of me time	*www.alittlebitofmetime.com*
Angels Den	*www.angelsden.com*
Artistry in Cocoa	*www.artistryincocoa.co.uk*
Carry-a-Bag	*www.carry-a-bag.com*
Chrysalis Promotions	*www.chrysalispromotions.com*
Corporate Mothers	*www.coachingmums.com*
Cyber Sec, The	*www.thecybersec.co.uk*
Doodlebugz	*www.doodlebugz.co.uk*
Ecoteriors	*www.ecoteriors.co.uk*
Enterprise Nation	*www.enterprisenation.com*
Exceptional Thinking	*www.exceptionalthinking.co.uk*
Freestyle Success	*www.freestylesuccess.com*
Fundamentals	*www.fundamentalsonline.co.uk*
FunkiJunk Jewellery Company, The	*www.funkijunkjewellery.co.uk*
GroBox Gardens Ltd	*www.groboxgardens.co.uk*
Hospitality Store	*www.hospitalitystore.co.uk*

I Can Do Better	www.icandobetter.co.uk
Izzy Lane	www.izzylane.co.uk
Living Clean	www.livingclean.co.uk
Mike Rimmer	www.crossrhythms.co.uk
Moo Marketing	www.moomarketing.co.uk
Music Bugs	www.musicbugs.co.uk
My Secret Kitchen	www.mysecretkitchen.co.uk
Nicecupofteaandasitdown.com	www.nicecupofteaandasitdown.com
Nikki Spencer	http://tinyurl.com/2ugh3n
Noolibird	www.noolibird.com
Pink Camellia	www.pinkcamellia.com
Pomegranate Public Relations	www.pom-pr.com
Popupology	www.popupology.co.uk
PortrayIt	www.portrayit.co.uk
San Sharma	www.sansharma.com
Shedworking	www.shedworking.co.uk
Smart Garden Offices	www.smartgardenoffices.co.uk
Soap and Bubble Company, The	www.soapandbubble.com
Tail-Swishing	www.tail-swishing.co.uk
Tots to France	www.totstofrance.co.uk

Travel Counsellors	*www.travelcounsellors.com*
Truly Madly Baby	*www.trulymadlybaby.co.uk*
Virgin Vie	*www.virginvieathome.com*
Wiggly Wigglers	*www.wigglywigglers.co.uk*
Words That sell	*www.wordsthatsell.co.uk*
Zheni Warner	*www.grapevinegallery.co.uk*

Templates

SWOT Analysis

STRENGTHS

What are my strengths?

WEAKNESSES

What are my weaknesses?

OPPORTUNITIES

What opportunities do I see?

THREATS

What are my threats?

Marketing plan

MEDIA

Press	
National press	*Insert your list of target titles here*
Regional & local press	*Insert your list of target titles here*
Trade press	*Insert your list of target titles here*

Radio

Insert programmes on which you'd like to appear

Television

Insert programmes on which you'd like to appear

Magazines

Insert list of target titles

Online

Websites	*Insert list of sites for reciprocal links*
Blogs	*Insert list of blogs on which you'll comment*

Press releases

Press hook stories	*Insert list of press stories for the year*
Image to attach?	*Yes/No*

OTHER

Events

Insert list of events to attend; networking and trade. Aim for speaking opportunities and what about hosting your own event too.

Awards

Insert list of awards relevant to your business.

NOTES

Press release

Headline

Attention grabbing headline.

First line

The first line is punchy and explains the what, who, why and where of the headline.

Facts and figures

Back up the headline and first sentence with facts and figures.

Your quote

Include a quote from you.

A quote from someone else

Can you include a quote from someone else? A happy customer, industry expert, or celebrity?

Call to action

End with a call to action. Where can people go to find out more/how to download the report/which site to visit to claim a free gift etc., etc.

Notes to editors

Include 'Notes to Editors' with brief details about you and your company.

Contact details

Remember to include contact details – your email address and telephone number.

Image

Attach a relevant and interesting image.

Admin to-do list

Inform the council (if required)	☐
Update insurance policy	☐
Do health & safety check	☐
Inform mortgage provider	☐
Tell the neighbours	☐
Any other business	

Technology healthcheck

Have you restarted your computer recently?	☐
Have you updated your software via Windows or Software update?	☐
Is your anti-virus software up-to-date?	☐
Have you backed up recently?	☐
Do you have a sufficiently cryptic password that you change regularly?	☐
Any other business	

Index